RAISING THE BAR: BUILDING AUTHENTIC RELATIONSHIPS

TRANSFORMING LEADERS IN THE CHURCH AND WORKPLACE

DR. GLORIA MILLER PERRIN
FOREWORD BY H. BEECHER HICKS, JR.

Unless otherwise indicated, Scripture quotations are taken from the New King James Version of the Bible.

Printed in the United States of America
2019 First Edition
10 9 8 7 6 5 4 3 2 1

Subject Index:
Miller Perrin, Gloria
Title: Raising the Bar: Building Authentic Relationships, Transforming Leaders in the Church and Workplace
1. Leadership 2. Church 3. Workplace 4. Christian 5. Inspirational 6. Personal Development

Library of Congress Card Catalog Number: 2019950531
Paperback ISBN: 978-0-578-56263-6
Cover Design: Pamela D. Spaulding - millerdesignsonline.com
Book Coach: Kim A. Rouse - covenantwithyou.com

GMP Ministries LLC
GMP Publishing
Website:www.leadersraisingthebar.com

Praises for Raising the BAR...

"The book, *Raising the Bar* by Dr. Gloria Miller Perrin expands the age-old leadership discussion in unique and different ways. In seven distinct sections, the text defines leadership styles and then challenges the reader to look introspectively, before seeking to build healthy relationships in the church and workplace environments. This concept aligns perfectly with Biblical principles in that we are called to love others as ourselves. This book will give you a better understanding of what it means to be a leader and will challenge you to be the most authentic leader that you could possibly be."

Pastor John K. Jenkins Sr.
First Baptist Church of Glenarden, MD

"I know of no one better to delve into the area of authentic relationships than

Dr. Gloria Miller-Perrin, a woman I've known for more than three decades, has demonstrated over and over the meaning of integrity, authenticity and Godly leadership. She does not seek the applause of men, nor women, but only the applause of God. Loyal, Faithful, and Authentic, she models 21st Century leadership. I highly commend *Raising the Bar* as a "must-read," for all who **lead**!"

Ambassador Suzan Johnson Cook
Former U.S. 3rd Ambassador-at-large for International Religious Freedom Appointed by President Barack Obama

"This book offers a valuable compendium of information and insights for modern-day leaders. Dr. Gloria Miller Perrin challenges us to deepen our understanding of emotional intelligence and other concepts that nurture the authenticity and awareness needed to enhance our effectiveness as leaders in the church and in the workplace. Anyone who leads or aspires to leadership will want to add *Raising the Bar* to their library."

Dr. Cheryl J. Sanders

Author of *Empowerment Ethics* and *Ministry at the Margins*

Professor of Christian Ethics at Howard University School of Divinity and Senior Pastor of Third Street Church of God in Washington, D.C.

"*Raising the Bar* is a tremendous book written by the distinguished, Reverend Dr. Gloria Miller Perrin. As a medical doctor, it is essential for me to help one achieve a healthier body. Additionally, I feel that it is equally important to develop a healthier mindset and lifestyle for ultimate achievement in any industry. This easy to follow book is a powerful platform towards creating a healthier, more authentic leader by utilizing a multitude of credible strategies. I am confident that any reader will garner the positive results for greater success by embracing *Raising The Bar* book. Congratulations, Dr. Miller Perrin!"

Melanye Maclin-Carroll, M.D. aka 'Dr. Mac'

Celebrity Dermatologist

"*Raising the Bar*, by Dr. Gloria Miller Perrin is a smart and pithy book focusing on the challenging and elusive concept of "authentic leadership". The book captures a wealth of leadership definitions and formulas and offers them in a practical format helpful for leaders at any level. The reader is pleasingly confronted with the author's passion for deep change in the leadership landscape as she explores leadership mishaps in an array of settings. The expectation is that through honest self-assessment and consistent implementation of espoused core values effective and sustained leadership success will be readily obtainable. By presenting a blended message calling for high integrated moral character, sound methodology, and consistent behavior one cuts through the noise and strips away the needless mystery surrounding authentic leadership. This is a value-packed guide, and an accessible read to underline and implement."

Dr. Cynthia Rembert James

Director of Education, Pastoral Staff

Potters House Dallas

"*Raising the Bar* is the new leadership blueprint for anyone seeking personal growth and development. Although authenticity is a trending buzz word, it is necessary to be a great leader. It requires us to be honest, transparent, and accountable at all times. Dr. Miller Perrin breaks down the process of building your authentic self into powerful, easy to remember acronyms to help keep you on track. There are several great ones, yet remaining true to your **CORE VALUES** resonated with me. If we espoused to live out our CORE VALUES as *Raising the Bar* challenges us to do, we will undoubtedly be better leaders and better human beings."

Dr. Johnny Parker

Author of *Turn the Page*

Adjunct Professor Johns Hopkins University

"Dr. Miller Perrin has written a remarkable book to help us all do better and be better. *Raising the Bar*, thoughtful, enlightening, elegantly written with clear knowledge and a path to better leadership and service. Dr. Perrin provides key techniques for people in all walks of life. This book can definitely be used across disciplines. *Raising the Bar* provides a blueprint for change and success—easy to read and practical."

Dorothy Bailey, Former Chair, Prince George's County Council

"In what I contend will be a landmark leadership book, Dr. Perrin dares to broach and encroach on the delicate and thus shunned leadership issues of the disingenuous, self-aggrandizing, and distant leader. This leader really doesn't like people but only what they can do for his professional ascend to power.

"Given to hospitality" is the qualification for Biblical leadership that far too many leaders conclude to be an unnecessary attribute for the ascendant leader. I'm just not sure how they missed the many passages of Scripture which recount Jesus, "hanging out" and "partying" with them even going to their homes for dinner.

In my forty years of full-time pastoral leadership, I've seen the number of relational leaders dwindling thus I'm encouraged that work is being written and *Raising the Bar* can help add to the discussion.

If you are only interested in another "feel good" book which will make you a better "leader" you can pass on this book. But if you sense the need to be more relational and authentic, get this book and buy one for your best friend, if you have one."

Pastor TL Rogers, Pastor Emeritus

The Triumphant Church

Raising the Bar is more than a book: It is an in-depth road map for anyone who may be conflicted about their leadership or trying to blend their spiritual and cultural selves with their leadership. The book focuses on responsiveness and common-sense approaches to the challenges of leadership and will clarify your mind, body and spirit connections to great leadership.

Raising the Bar is a gut-wrenching look at the power of relationships; closing your character gaps and forcing you to reflect on your past leadership choices and relationships.

When you finish reading Raising the Bar you will answer two questions: What Am I Here to Do and What Impact Will I Make?

Sandra R. Fowler

Commercial Real Estate Executive

"Dr. Gloria Perrin has created a vital tool for senior leaders to strengthen the leadership culture of their church. Her insightful wisdom, memorable acronyms, and practical applications will help any pastor build transparency and authenticity amongst their leaders. Such an environment will enhance the morale and production of your team, and make your leadership more effective."

Dr. Bobby Manning

Pastor; First Baptist Church of District Heights, MD

Author, *Saving our Sons: Effectively Engaging Young Men of Color*

"*Raising the Bar* by Dr. Gloria Miller Perrin helped me identify what was missing from what I was taught about good leadership. Much has been written about leadership traits and skills, but the effects that the ethical or unethical behavior of leaders has on their relationships with their followers is rarely discussed or analyzed. Additionally, it is rare to find tools to help leaders identify whether their personal styles are producing authentic relationships that lead to greater productivity and success. Through the results of Dr. Perrin's extensive research, *Raising the Bar* emphasizes the significance of knowing and being true to yourself and others in order to bring value to the team you are leading. It will guide you through your own personal journey toward building and maintaining authentic relationships. I highly recommend this book to all leaders who want to increase their potential for success personally and professionally."

Jacquie Gales Webb

Multimedia Host, Peabody Award-winning Producer, and Director of Initiatives in Music, Production, and Organizational Collaboration

"Whether you are a leader in the Church a para-church organization or the corporate world, Miller-Perrin provides a clear, concise picture of what authentic leadership looks like and how to achieve it. The author invites each of us with specific tools to take a personal inventory of the positive and negative aspects of our own leadership style to determine if we measure up to the challenge. Most importantly, she provides concrete steps to help us navigate toward the authenticity needed for truly effective leadership."

Dr. Estrelda Alexander, President

William Seymour College

"Raising the Bar will strike a timely chord with any reader, especially a leader who is striving for authentic leadership in all areas of life. The book outlines the characteristics of authentic leadership, real and attainable, in stark contrast to the current environment we live in today which is marked by moral and societal decay. Dr. Miller Perrin has penned an important book that should send any leader or those aspiring to leadership into a time of serious soul-searching, culminating in the question – *Am I an authentic leader?*"

Reverend Esther L. Gordon

Associate Pastor

Department Head, Education and Training Ministries

Dedication

To our past leaders who stood the test of time, vigilant to their assignments and whose shoulders we now stand on.

To our present leaders who are demonstrating what it means to lead and not compromise their values and remain true to themselves by Raising the BAR.

To our emerging leaders who are picking up the mantel and are blazing a path for generations to come.

Acknowledgments

First, I honor God as He continues to remind me that He is able to do exceedingly abundantly above all that I can think or imagine. The completion of this book is truly an exceeding and abundant moment, for which I truly thank God.

Secondly, to Henry Perrin my husband who lets me be me by loving me with unconditional love. To our children who we love so much and are proud of who they are becoming: Darrin and Pamela (the best Graphics designer in the world) Robert and Pamela, Pierre and Tracey, and Joshua Perrin our son, who lights up our house every day. All of Henry's sisters and brother, nieces, nephews, and grandchildren. All of them who have supported me with love during this process in ways they will never know. To all the Perrin/Rogers clan so many I can't count. I am so blessed to be in the number. To my nieces Rhonda, Lynn, Australia, and their children, I thank God for you.

To my circle of friends (for which I have been blessed with many) who are too numerous to name in this space. You know who you are. To Karlatta and Yvonne who have been my friends for over 50 years, as we walk through thick and thin from high school to now. To my cohorts at Regent in the doctoral program; Anita and Fa2 who together we burned the midnight oil, they were the wind beneath my wings as we made it to the finish line. For that, I will be forever grateful. My three Exhale Sisters; Dr. Carmen Lattimore, Dr. Stephanie Stratford, and Dr. Kelly Hayes they too have supported me all the way, as we shared times together letting our hair down; knowing that whatever happens with the Exhale Sisters stays with the Exhale Sisters. Our four-hour monthly luncheons and yearly weekend get-a-ways fueled a fire in me, not to quit. I was energized to get back to work on this project after some timeouts with them.

To some of the most brilliant women God has allowed to cross my path: Dr. Estrelda Alexander, Ambassador Suzan Johnson Cook, and Dr. Thomasina Portis, they are all examples for me of what excellence looks like, as they have carved their paths to be on the World Stage.

To my pastor John K. Jenkins Sr. and First Lady Trina Jenkins who often saw more in me than I saw in myself giving me an opportunity to serve at the First Baptist Church of Glenarden for almost 20 years. To all of our leadership. Shout out to Elder Williams Jones who thought it not robbery, to read through my manuscript and share his insights. To Pastor Duane Dickerson and Rev. Cynthia Terry, who always cheered me in word and deed. To our staff, I say a heartfelt thank-you. To my ministerial colleagues, many who encouraged me on this journey, believing that God will use my work to his glory. Many prematurely gave me the title "Doc" long before it was due. I am clear it does take a village to write a book. For that I am humbled.

"This is the Lord's doing and it is marvelous in my sight."

TABLE OF CONTENTS

Foreword

By

H. Beecher Hicks, Jr., D. Min.

Dr. Gloria Miller-Perrin has provided readers with an introspective word into the world of leadership which has merit for those of us who seek guidance and direction in this arena. This writing is particularly needed for those who seek to live the authentic life as well as to expose those we lead toward a paradigm of leadership that is above the pedantic and the ordinary. Dr. Miller-Perrin takes the reader to a level of introspection that will not permit us to be comfortable with the common and in so doing prepares us and requires of us a higher level of leadership that lifts us to the highest levels of "transparency and ethical decision-making" in spite of internal or external pressures.

The work of high-level leadership is necessary at all levels of our lives and of our organizations, our families and our churches, as well. High-level leadership achieves several purposes. First, Perrin assumes in this writing the necessary development of common vision and goals; second, the construction of authentic and meaningful relationships and, third, the eradication of love/hate relationships which tend toward the destruction of leaders who are empowered toward the calling that is prescient and revealed in their lives.

The author defines "leader as one "who has the capacity to influence followers who believe that the stated mission is important and attainable. Without such a stated and accepted mission, any effort toward leadership will be met with failure. Moreover, we will be passengers on a bus with no agreements on just where we are headed or how soon we will arrive. One has only to look at the recent political antics of our current national leadership and beyond to see the truth of these words; quite similarly, one has only to look to churches as well as a vast variety of religious organizations that need to be led to the inarguable necessity for the raising of the bar as our only hope for our future. Stated differently, for leadership to be transformational, leaders must first be transformed.

Our thanks to Dr. Miller-Perrin for her insightful and thoughtful journey into this arena which can only eventuate into stronger leadership, stronger organizations and greater integrity among all of us who seek to be leaders.

Dr. H. Beecher Hicks, Jr.

Introduction

In Search of the Real McCoy

"Authenticity is your most precious commodity as a leader."
— Marcus Buckingham

The word "authentic" has become the buzzword of our day. Everyone is looking for the real deal. The Millennials call it "Keeping it 100." More and more people are looking for authenticity with those they encounter. The desire for genuineness is evident whether building platonic or professional relationships. It doesn't matter how rich, famous or talented a person may be, superficiality and insincerity are bound to be uncovered. There is a growing dissatisfaction with the online portrayals of sleek and airbrushed photos, misrepresented personalities, and luxurious lifestyles paraded to the masses with zero truth or substance.

What type of leader do you strive to be? The paradox is that there are two types of leaders that you will likely encounter—authentic or inauthentic. All too often leaders attempt to play both sides of the fence. They start off with good intentions in their leadership role to build a following and earn a good reputation. Then something happens along the way and they start mimicking someone else and engaging in activities that demonstrate a lack of character and integrity.

Authentic leaders are those that are striving to be open, honest, and straightforward. I use the word "striving" because *none* of us have arrived. It takes daily effort and keen self-awareness. Authentic leaders are not willing to compromise their values and beliefs. Their behavior is consistent whether they are in the gym, on the golf course, in the pulpit, or in the boardroom. They know themselves and are comfortable in their own skin. Although usually charismatic, these leaders are more concerned about their character than charisma. Transparency and ethical decision-making are important to them regardless of internal or external pressures.

Inauthentic leaders, on the other hand, are full of pretense. These leaders are comfortable shading the truth and then distracting you from seeing their fingers crossed behind their backs. They spend the majority of their time pretending to be someone they are not, in an effort to satisfy their own self-interest, usually for greed or notoriety. Inauthentic leaders are like chameleons; willing to change their behavior and character to fall in line with the majority or whatever is trending. They tell people what they want to hear and conform to the expectations of others to gain acceptance and favor, all while knowing that they are not going to follow through on their promises. These types of leaders have no problem lying to make others feel good.

Knowing that this paradox exists amongst too many of our leaders, the question becomes what can be done to stop the deception, dishonesty, and personality duplicity that keeps leaders trapped in a dysfunctional cycle? Especially since there have been numerous church and workplace scandals occurring that have heightened our consciousness to the fact that self-interest unchecked by moral reasoning can result in destructive behaviors. These destructive behaviors not only eventually destroy the lives of those who participate, but ultimately impacts the lives of thousands of innocent individuals as the negative outcomes trickle down and crash through families, communities, and ultimately society.

It is imperative that leaders in the church and the workplace start to explore what is needed to create the best blueprint to improve the health of their organizations. As we are pondering this all too familiar dilemma, I would raise the question, could "authenticity" be an antidote to our current leadership crisis in government, corporations, entertainment, the media, and elsewhere?

If leaders in the church and the workplace make a deliberate effort to becoming authentic to "Raise the Bar" in leading others, leaders must first be willing to look in the mirror. They must take a serious inventory of themselves and ask, Am I living out my life as the "Real Me?" What are my purpose and my passion as a leader? What is my underlying motivation to do what I do? I am persuaded that if leaders are not real and honest with themselves, they can never be real and honest with others.

Since none of us have arrived in completing our authentic disposition, leaders need to be on an intentional developmental journey, striving every day to walk the walk and talk the talk. Paul spoke this to Timothy, his young protégée, and provided hard-edge direction to help Timothy understand that sound doctrine will only get him so far if it isn't lived out. *Let no one despise your youth, but be an example to the believers in words, in conduct, in love, in spirit, in faith, in purity.*[1] The bottom line is that a leader's beliefs do not make him a better leader—only his behavior counts.

My goal in writing *Raising the Bar* is not to place blame, call out, or criticize leaders. Instead, my intent is just the opposite. I hope to advance the concept and the construct of authenticity as it relates to the leader's behavior that comes from making ethical and unethical decisions. I desire to revisit the paradigm for leadership development to help leaders overcome some of the challenges that lead to a disconnect between followers. *Raising the Bar* provides new tools for a leaders' toolbox that should propel a path forward to move the leader's relationships to another authentic and engaging level.

Authentic leaders not only motivate others in their sphere of influence, but they also empower their constituents to become better leaders. My aim is to invite you on a journey with me, asking and answering hard questions that could change the trajectory of inauthentic behavior amongst leaders in the church and the workplace. A key starting point will be framed by asking:

- *Why are so many leaders experiencing a relationship divide among their team members as they work toward a common vision and goals for their organization?*
- *What is the missing ingredient(s) in these organizations divide and conquer encounters as leaders seek to build authentic relationships?*
- *Why have leaders developed love/hate relationships with their colleagues as they seek to be true to themselves and the calling on their lives?*

There are no easy answers to these questions, however, I believe small steps can start the process. With seven being the number of completion, *Raising the Bar* is organized into seven parts to highlight the key area's leaders can focus on to gradually build upon their authentic journey. In the early chapters, we will define leadership, leadership styles, and the characteristics of authentic versus inauthentic leaders. We later dive into core values, building strong relationships, and the importance of emotional intelligence. At the end of each chapter there are "Authentic Check-up" questions intended for individual reflection or to facilitate group discussion.

Finally, I want to discharge the notion that this book is a complete representation of the subject matter. The societal impact of authentic and inauthentic behavior amongst leaders has been ongoing for centuries. I have researched leadership a great deal during my doctoral studies and my endeavor is to expand the conversation and offer new perspectives and resources to help leaders develop and grow personally and professionally. At the end of the day, no matter how you slice it, when you know better, you do better. The time has come for all of us to raise the leadership bar.

PART I

One Size Does Not Fit All

"I'm sure the Pharaoh was a great guy, but I've got my own leadership style."

CHAPTER 1

LEADERSHIP 101

Defining Leadership

"If you call yourself a leader and no one is following you, then you are just talking a walk."
— *Anonymous*

Are you a leader? The terms "leader" and "leadership" will continue to be trending buzzwords in our daily lives whether you look inside the church environment or the corporate workplace. Leaders create the organization's vision, as well as inspire and motivate individuals to achieve greater outcomes. Companies with strong leadership tend to have greater employee satisfaction and high productivity. John Maxwell, one of the most highly regarded leadership experts of our time, once said, "Any endeavor you undertake that involves people will live or die depending on leadership because everything rises and falls on leadership."

From a historical perspective, leadership has its roots since the beginning of civilization. It was a topic of conversation during the days of Confucius, Plato, Machiavelli, Aristotle, and other philosophers. More importantly, leadership is described in the beginning of the Hebrew Bible in Genesis. There are volumes of books, newspapers, magazines and scholarly articles available today on various aspects of leadership. Fortunately, in this 21st Century, leadership has evolved from an authoritarian style to methods and behaviors that involve a more relational aspect in the church and the workplace environment. This new approach has been proven to help teams feel empowered, encouraged, and supported in their personal, professional and spiritual growth.

The word "leader," means to show the way, to guide. [2] It has its origins in the English word "leden," which means to travel or also show the way. Bernard M. Bass an American psychologist defines leadership as "an interaction between two or more members of a group that involves a structuring or restructuring of a situation and the perceptions and expectations of the members." [3]

Being a leader is not a walk in the park. Leadership often means making sacrifices beyond what your initial thoughts were before taking the position. Accepting the leadership assignment is a summons to do the heavy lifting by agreeing to take responsibility for the outcome of others. It is true that the buck stops with the leader, without exceptions, and without excuses. Leaders must be willing to make hard-hitting decisions in the face of criticism and are willing to engage in conflict even though they may have to stand alone.

As a leader, you can't take people further than you have gone yourself, especially if you are more concerned about what people think or seeking validation from others. If leaders allow people to control them by being a people pleaser, then they are not leading, instead, they are following and being lead. Many are willing to adorn the title and perks of leadership, but few are willing to pay the price to lead.

Leader versus Manager Debate

I've researched scholars like Warren Bennis who believe that too many of our organizations are "over-managed and under-led."[4] Bennis and many others in the field view this issue as a contributing factor in the debate as to which role is more important—management versus leadership. Some behavioral scientists say that it is the manager who is more important since the role involves developing strategies, organizing and coordinating efforts. Leaders, are there to inspire and motivate after the team has carried out the manager's instruction. Then the leader should eventually move those followers to the next level of success.

An additional understanding prevalent in today's culture is that leaders create change, while managers create stability. Both managers and leaders are needed in our organizational life, as they operate in their giftings and context. So, the question is not who is more important because both are essential. The question should be, how can leaders and managers work together more efficiently to achieve greater outcomes? The truth of the matter is that not all managers are leaders and not all leaders are managers. Of course, there are overlapping and gray areas to leadership and quiet as it's kept, some leaders can function effectively in both roles.

Believe it or not, the top search engines reveal thousands of definitions for "leadership" even though it is such a familiar and overly-used term. Think of leadership as a common designator with a myriad of meanings, because leadership can be innately difficult and hard to define. The truth is, leadership is multifaceted so be open to various meanings as opposed to clinging to one definition which may become problematic, as there is no one-size-fits-all definition.

Here are a few leadership definitions to consider:

- Leadership is having a clear sense of mission and purpose.
- Leadership is serving.
- Leadership is helping individuals or groups to achieve goals.
- Leadership is leading with moral integrity.
- Leadership is transformational.
- Leaderships is center on principles.
- Leadership is relational.

As you can see, the list and your personal list could go on and on. However, there is one thing for sure; leadership is not a solo act. There must be at least one or more persons involved before it can be accurately called leadership. As the superhero Batman can attest, with all of his incredible gadgets, he still needed Robin to help stop the bad guys. These two were the original Dynamic Duo in the comics. I've heard it said many times, "if no one is following you, then you are just talking a walk." It all boils down to the first step of being effective in leadership is that you must convince others that you have the capability to lead them on a fruitful journey. Therefore, I will use my working definition of leadership.

A leader is one who has the capacity to influence followers who believe that the stated mission is important and attainable. This person creates persuasive outcomes using his or her skill sets and foresight to influence, inspire and raise the performance of the followers to get positive results.

Leadership Characteristics

"It's no coincidence that the words influence and influenza come from the same root word. Real leaders are contagious. People "catch" what they have."

— ***Michael Hyatt***

The ability to influence is a vital skill set that every leader needs to acquire for positive outcomes. Small, if any, sustainable results will be achieved if the leader is not able to influence his follower's thoughts and actions to bring the leader's desired outcomes to fruition. Another way to sum up a great leadership characteristic is about being a change agent through influencing. Leadership is the tool that motivates and inspires individuals to see things in themselves that they would not otherwise see.

At the rudimentary stage, leadership capacity and influence is about getting followers to come to a place of agreement and submission to recognize key tasks, targets and goals. The keywords here are "capacity" and "influence" for defining leadership. Other renowned leaders have described critical leadership characteristics as:

"Leadership: The capacity and will to rally people to a common purpose together with the character that inspires confidence and trust."

— Bernard Montgomery

"Leadership is the capacity to translate vision into reality."

— Warren Bennis

Leadership: "a process whereby an individual influences a group of individuals to achieve a common goal." [5]

— P. G. North

"Leadership is the capacity to influence others through inspiration, motivation by passion generated by vision, produced by a conviction, ignited by a purpose."

— Myles Munroe

When a person serves under a great leader, they never leave the same way they came; they are a better version of themselves. The Apostle Paul in the Bible was a great leader. "He called the disciples together and encouraged them by lifting their spirits… charging them with fresh hope.[6] Hope becomes a tool throughout the Bible that leaders use to inspire their followers. From a historical observation, Napoleon Bonaparte presented interesting dynamics to his leadership abilities including, hope.

"A leader is a dealer in hope."

— Napoleon Bonaparte

Napoleon: A Dealer of Hope

By Mark Billings[7]

Napoleon is arguably the first modern leader in that he spoke directly to his people. Using the press and the media with great mastery, he initiated a revolution in the techniques of communication, manipulation, and power. Napoleon understood quite well the art and science of psychology and how to get others to do what he wanted them to do. In short, he was a genius at self-promotion, a quite effective propagandist. No great (or infamous) leader since Napoleon has neglected these techniques at human manipulation. As with many of his military tactics and strategies, Napoleon was not necessarily the inventor of these techniques; rather, he was the first one to apply them in a systematic fashion.

From early on in his career, Napoleon set in place a deliberate and sophisticated communications apparatus aimed to boost the morale of the French army and general populace and, as a corollary, his own reputation. Napoleon employed effectively a variety of media, from inspirational speeches to the troops to the famous Bulletins of the Grande Armée posted in cities across France. The underlying theme of Napoleon's communications campaign was a message of hope and optimism for the French people and the army. Napoleon was the one who would preserve the gains of the Revolution. His personal leadership was portrayed as central to the success of the French Republic and Empire.

He was also a commander who knew how to speak to his men. On the eve of the First Italian Campaign, Napoleon launched the following challenge to his troops:

"Soldiers! You are naked and ill-fed. No glory shines upon you. The government owes you a great deal, but it can give you nothing. Your patience and courage do you honor and give you neither worldly goods nor glory. I shall lead you into the most fertile plains on Earth. There, you shall find great cities and rich provinces. There, you shall find honor, glory, riches. Soldiers of the Army of Italy! Could courage and constancy possibly fail you?"

Napoleon and his rag-tag army quickly won four successive battles!

Every leader needs to be clear that influencing others has nothing to do with manipulating, bribing or bargaining, at least not in authentic leadership relationships. If a leader does not have the capacity to influence her followers without manipulation, she will ultimately lose her followers when her true intent and purpose are revealed. Genuine character and integrity will rear its head when leaders are faced with adversity, so leaders rise or fall are bound to be in the spotlight.

At the end of the day, the leader needs the cooperation and commitment from her followers to bring the vision and aspirations into reality. No leader is an island, so buy-in from followers is paramount. I also want to make this point clear, just because you may not have the title of leader in your church or organization, you are a leader. Everyone is a leader and responsible for their actions in their own environment. Leadership is about influence and we all have influence over our own lives and some aspects of other's lives. Leadership is a dichotomy. There is a good, productive side, as well as a bad, damaging side. Which side are you on?

Chapter 1: Leadership 101

Authentic Check-up

1. In one sentence share your definition of what it means to be a leader.

2. Name one male and one female leader from history that has influenced your life. Share something about them as a leader that stood out to you.

3. Name one male and female leader in your present environment that has influenced your life. Share something about them that stood out to you.

4. Do you consider yourself a leader? If yes, why? If no, why not?

CHAPTER 2

LEADERSHIP STYLES

"The first responsibility of a leader is to define reality. The last is to say thank you. In between, the leader is a servant."
— Max De Pree

When it comes to leadership styles there is no one approach to getting the job done. Research shows that there are many similar traits and behavioral approaches leaders bring to their positions, but since everyone has different backgrounds and experiences, no two leaders' methods are identical. During the past decade, different leadership styles have been written about to bring this issue to the mainstream. As a result, a new paradigm of leadership has evolved. There is a discernible correlation between leadership styles and the effect it has on building positive or negative relationships.

Since there are several leadership styles, a leader's style could evolve over time based on the situation and the number of followers. There is also the possibility that there may not be one leadership style that will ultimately build authentic relationships, but a combination or overlapping of styles. As leaders, it is essential that you identify your style(s) to become more conscious of how you interact with people. Your style is what gives you influence and credibility to lead your followers.

From my research, there are five types of leadership styles that appear to be the most prevalent in today's church and workplace cultures. They are Charismatic, Transactional, Transformational, Servant, and Authentic. In each of these styles, there is a relational impact that can determine a leader's success in connecting with followers. However, I want to make it clear that certain styles alone do not secure relational success. The overriding question becomes are there components in each style that will help or hinder in building authentic relationships as the leaders and followers work together? It is clear from my research that despite the leadership style if the leader has no intention to build relationships, there will not be significant rewards produced for the leader, the organization, nor its followers.

Charismatic Leadership

The theory of charismatic leadership emerged in the 1900's borrowing from the term "charisma" from the New Testament in the Bible. Charisma referred to an impartation of the Holy Spirit as a gift from God when individuals committed their lives to Jesus. Max Weber, a German sociologist, is credited with introducing the term in 1947 in his work in the management field. Weber described these leaders as having "exceptional qualities, a charisma that enabled them to motivate followers to achieve outstanding performance." [8]

A charismatic leader leans heavy on their engaging personality and their persuasiveness which does not necessarily include a methodology or a structure. This style of leadership does not always work well for organizations that have inflexible formats and needs processes and procedures to function. These leaders operate more out of courage and convictions.

Charismatic leadership can be described from at least two vantage points. First, being present in today's complex organizations as supportive, sensitive, nurturing, and considerate. Charismatic leaders are widely known as strong motivators that positively influence their followers around mutual objectives. They exude confidence and almost never express self-doubt, at least not in public. Charismatic leaders are usually excellent communicators, in every sense of the word. They are so eloquent in their presentation that they can formulate an appealing vision that provokes fierce reactions in those who follow. They communicate from deep-seated passions. It has been said that Charismatic leaders can charm themselves.

In addition, Charismatic leaders are known by their extraordinary accomplishments that serve as an inspiration to others to function at similarly remarkable levels. They have powerful personalities that people want to follow. These types of leaders move outside of the box and will go beyond expectations in leading and driving innovation. Charismatic leaders are among the early adopters when it comes to innovation, especially in times of crisis when change is needed. They are very optimistic looking toward the future, seeking ways to bring about advancement and making the world a better place. Charismatic leaders are orientated to risk-taking because they have the foresight and are prone to be futurists.

The second description of a charismatic leader comes from traditional stereotypes as one who is uncompromising, demanding, controlling, and disparaging. This speaks to the downside of this type of leadership. These leaders are often known as being self-absorbed and self-serving. Charismatic leaders are described as representing themselves endowed with a special power, but essentially an unstable force that emerged in times of stress. From the idea of being endowed by God with a special talent, as it was originally understood from the Bible, the emerging conceptualizing of charismatic leaders were identified as one who took it upon himself or herself to convince others that their talents were indeed supernatural in some way. Often their flaws are ignored, at the same time their strong line of reasoning is accentuated by their followers. Charismatic leaders are often described to have narcissistic tendencies. They fail to delegate and are unpredictable as they deal with inner conflicts. Charismatic leaders can have difficulties in making decisions and are often insensitive to others; without realizing the effects of their behavior.

Other dark sides of Charismatic leadership is too often they are unwilling to admit their mistakes, therefore they are unable to learn from them. There is a level of arrogance that is developed with their success whereby they become less and less approachable to their followers. These leaders often assert themselves above the law, falling into moral and ethical disobedience. These behaviors tend to limit the leader's overall productivity particularly in building authentic relationships. See Table 1.

Table 1

Name	Example
Dr. Martin Luther King Jr.	United thousands of people and led them to a peaceful fight against racial discrimination and inequality.
Barack Obama	The 44th President of the United States was able to bring together Americans and foreigners to work for a cause greater than themselves. He was considered one of the best speech givers in American presidential history. He was able to attract cross cultures of numerous religious sectors. Obama was not perfect, but arguably he was one of the most extraordinary presidents of the United States.

Name	Example
Steve Jobs – Inventor of the iPhone	Widely known as arrogant, dictatorial, and mean-spirited. Not known for consensus building, gave blunt delivery of criticisms., He exerted control over every aspect of the business in the quest for perfection. His way or the highway, yet he was a great leader when it came to innovation.
Jim Warren Jones	American religious cult leader initiated and was responsible for a mass suicide and murder in Jonestown, Guyana. 918 persons died 304 of them were children

Transactional Leadership

The second style is transactional leadership which appears to be the most prevalent method of leadership observed in many of today's organizations. James McGregor Burns first identified this style by positing that transactional leaders focus on the specific interactions between leaders and followers in order to maintain the status quo. These transactions are a method by which an individual gains influence and sustain it over time by offering a reward in exchange for accomplishing goals and objectives. The process is based on reciprocity, "what have you done for me lately."

B.M. Bass describes the Transactional Leader relationship as, "The leader and the followers agree on what the follower needs to do to be rewarded or to avoid punishment. If the follower does agree, the leader arranges to reward the follower, or the leader does not impose aversive reinforcement such as correction, reproof, penalization or withdrawal of authorization to continue."[9]

Transactional leaders are "rules and order" personalities who run more of a military management style. Their focus is on results at any cost. Often, they put tasks over people. Transactional leaders give followers something they want, and the followers will give the leaders something they want—it is a typical quid pro quo exchange. This can be appealing to a self-interested follower seeking to appease her needs rather than what is best for the group. In addition, the contractual nature of this leadership style focuses on controlling followers. Transactional leaders function best when their followers are motivated by the rewards and penalties method. These leaders are reactive rather than proactive.

I believe there is a place for transactional leadership. It is not all bad and can work in many situations. Especially for followers who are motivated by the existing structure of the organization and initiative is not encouraged. Transactional leadership works well where there is a requirement for recurring tasks and short-term goals are quickly realized. For most people, cash and benefits can be effective persuaders for completing a task. The truth is that there is a significant number of people who are only concerned about doing their job to reap whatever rewards are available. The job is a means to an end— to pay the bills.

Finally, when Transactional Leadership stands alone, the downside may outweigh the good in comparison to other leadership styles. It is this type of leadership where the emphasis is always on the effects of the budget, event-driven, and product-driven over people. Thus, from my perspective, transactional leadership styles lack authentic relationship building with the followers, as there is no sense of personal care and human touch involved. The contingent reinforcement aspect of the transactional leadership implies that the follower is hindered from fully participating in the leader-follower relationships because it is one-sided. See table 2.

Table 2:

Name:	**Example:**
Margaret Thatcher (Labeled the Iron Lady) Prime Minister of England	Described as a controlling, one who strives for power and authority. Taking charge of everything and having full control over every decision. Uncompromising politics in that she believed in what she believes in. She was the first female leader to become a Prime Minister.
Bill Gates	In the early days of Microsoft, He would be described as a powerful and strict leader. Very tough-minded, task-oriented and held strict control of the organization. At the beginning stages of the company, his focus was more on achievements than comfort. When he realized his cofounder was not carrying his weight due to health challenges, Gates was cruel in pushing him out of the company. He was known for being rude, harsh and sometimes flippant of ideas from his team. During the developmental phases of the company, his supremacy in the transactional leadership style contributed to his remarkable progression showing that there is a place for transactional leadership style in becoming successful. However, in his later years, many would view him displaying a softer side.

Name:	Example:
Vince Lombardi – Football Coach	He took on the approach of telling rather than asking. It was more about showing the players what he wanted them to do and expecting them to perform every time. He did not entertain responses, there was an expectation that his way was the only way to accomplish the task. He believed in the quest for excellence and flawlessness was the only way to be successful in the National Football League. During his time as coach of the Green Bay Packers, he won six NFL Championship, two Super Bowls and was named NFL Coach of the year twice. His authoritative military history was his way of forming the team.

Transformational Leadership

Leadership is the catalyst for transforming the lives of people in the church and workplace. Transformational leadership gained prominence in James McGregor Burns' book, *Leadership,* in 1978. Burns identified both transactional and transformational styles of leadership. You were either one or the other, and it appears Burns viewed transformational was better. Burns writes, "Transformational leadership is a comprehensive approach that strives to change or transform followers to transcend their own short-term needs for long-term self-development, the good of the group, the organization, and society. Contrasting to other leadership styles, transformational leadership is totally about introducing change in the organization versus keeping the status quo."[10]

There is agreement in the field that Burns' conceptualizing of transforming leadership was seminal in providing a framework for understanding transforming leaders. According to Burns, "A transforming leader looks for potential motives in followers, seeks to satisfy higher needs, and engages the full person of the followers. The result of transforming leadership is a relationship of mutual stimulation and elevation that converts followers into leaders and may convert leaders into moral agents."[11]

For leaders that are transformational it about assisting followers in finding their value, potential, and purpose in life. In helping followers find their value, transformational leaders search for behaviors in followers that bring out the top qualities of that person. When it comes to followers accepting challenging assignments, transformational leaders are willing to let followers know that if they make mistakes, it can be chalked up to the learning process without fear of consequences, which is quite different from transactional relationships.

As it relates to potential, transformational leaders are often willing to move followers to a higher position in the organization before the follower has earned the credentials. This kind of promotional decision is solely based on the potential the leader sees in the follower. Transformational leaders are instrumental in facilitating the process for followers to identify their purpose. They inspire followers to come to a clear and concise understanding of the reason why they do what they do, essentially knowing why they were placed on the earth. Purpose fuels the reason why we get out of bed in the morning. Mark Twain said; "The two most important days in your life are the day you are born, and the day you find out why."

As I reflected on the transformational style of leadership, it is clear that this approach can help and not hinder building authentic relationships. It can also become a great platform for individuals and organizations to transform through modeling mutual supportive measures.

Leaders are authentically transformational when they increase awareness of what is right, good, and important to all parties involved in the workplace relationship.

Transformational leaders are always in the mode of communicating an inspiring vision to their followers of what can happen now and in the future. These leaders challenge their followers by empowering them to think out of the box to do more than they ever believed possible. At the end of the day, transformational leaders assist followers in moving to higher levels on the ladder of self-esteem and self-actualization in their quest to be successful and authentic. See Table 3.

Table 3:

Name	Example
Nelson Mandela, the first Black president of South Africa.	A positive thinker, could see the big picture, focus on goals and mission beyond himself. He had remarkable endurance, grit and determination, humility, hopefulness, and patience. He was able to motivate and inspire people into action. He had strong ethical and moral values. He never gave up despite 27 years being in imprisoned.
Oprah Winfrey, American Media proprietor, actress, businesswoman, and philanthropist.	She affects change in a positive way and inspires others at the same time. She is open to new experiences, exercising fairness to others, she cares about people beyond her inner circle. She has the charisma and confidence to influence other people. She encourages followers to be creative and innovative. She places great value on people as she seeks to motivate them.

Name	Example
Mark Zuckerberg, CEO Facebook	Described as encouraging and aggressive. Always open to suggestions. He focuses on building relationships and does not show that he wants to be in control of everything. He is sensitive to his people and encourages group relationships. He works hard on correcting his mistakes and learning from them.

Servant Leadership

The fourth style is servant leadership. In the early 1970s Robert Greenleaf, founder of the Servant Leadership Movement, was given credit for initiating the current interest in this style. Greenleaf does not necessarily write for the Christian world, but he developed an approach to this leadership style in his book *Servant Leadership: A Journey into the Nature of Legitimate Power and Greatness.* Greenleaf shares this comment: "Business leaders need to serve society more constructively than merely increasing profits for the company. Businesses should exist as much to provide meaningful work to the customer."

While, Greenleaf does not confess to be a Christian, nor does he build his case from a scriptural point of view, his thoughts have solid altruistic and ethical themes. In the book *Being Leader,* Aubrey Malphurs writes about Greenleaf, "Primary theme, and that of others with a similar position is that the leader/follower relationship is central to ethical leadership in our world." He argues that servant leaders are attentive to the needs and concerns of their followers. Servant Leaders see themselves as responsible for taking care of and nurturing their followers. These leaders endeavor to get it right in their interaction with others. One of the factors to point out is that their approach does not change depending on the situation. Servant leaders remain steadfast despite obstacles that may occur. Their goal is to always serve others first.

Servant leadership remains an intuitive-based theory because little empirical data on servant-leader's behavior exists. Nonetheless, the expression is more than just words. Most church leaders can fully embrace the servant leadership style because it is akin to the example Jesus showed to the church in the way He functioned. Servant leadership models the highest form of behavior that values people and makes it clear that organizational results are secondary outcomes. Greenleaf's leadership principles are undeniably constructed on biblical concepts whether he admits to it or not.

To see what servant leadership looks like in the real world, Hans Finzel answers the question in his book *The Top Ten Mistakes Leaders Make*:

"Servant leadership is about caring for others more than for ourselves. It is about compassion for everyone who serves the group. It enriches everyone, not just those at the top. Servant leadership requires us to sit and weep with those who weep within our organizations. It requires getting down and dirty when hard work has to be done. There is nothing in my organization that anyone does that I should not be willing to do myself if it promotes the good of us all."[12]

On the other side of the coin, let's look at what servant leadership is not. Aubrey Malphurs summarizes this thought when he said, "There are four common misconceptions about servant leadership: It is about doing ministry for others, being passive, focusing on the leader's weakness and ignoring the leader's own needs." [13] The principles of Servant

Leadership are clear as to why the Scripture teaches us in Matthew 22-37-39 – b part; " And the second is similar: Love your neighbor as yourself." Servant Leaders need to take care of themselves in order to be available to take care of others. See table 4.

Table 4:

Name	Example
Jesus Christ	For those who are Christians, Jesus is the greatest example of Servant Leadership. The Bible teaches that Jesus forfeited his majesty to come from Heaven to earth to reveal the love of God to His followers. It was done through the attributes of being a Servant Leader. In Mark 10:45 the Scripture reads "For even the Son of man did not come to be served, but to serve, and give his life for a ransom for many. Jesus teaches through the Scriptures that a real servant leader does not seek service for themselves, does not aim to do his own will and does not promote himself. A strong example of servanthood was when Jesus put a towel around his waist and washed the feet of the disciples.
Mother Teresa	Was recognized throughout the world for her service to the people of India. She refused praise for her work. When she was awarded the Nobel Peace Prize, she turned the opportunity to have a banquet and asked that the money to be given to the poor.

Name	Example
Mahatma Gandhi	He stood up to the British officials during his time. He believed that serving others was the best way to humble yourself. He demonstrates peaceful protest. Through pressure and time, his ideas won out, and he was able to free his country from colonialism. Dr. Martin Luther King modeled his protest movement after Gandhi.
Eleanor Roosevelt	Served as a role model for First Lady of the United States. Her work in Human Rights transformed what was expected of a First Lady. She played a crucial role in shaping the United Nations Declaration of Human Rights.
Truett Cathy – Founder of Chick-Fil-A	He stood for steadfast principles when it came to customer service in his restaurants. Many believe that he produced a mentality of Servant Leaderships. He focused on charitable contributions that his company would make by helping foster homes for abused and neglected children. While there is some controversy about Cathy's political views, not many can argue that his employee's customer service is at the highest quality and few restaurants of this order can match it.

Authentic Leadership

Finally, and of interest, as it relates to this discussion, is the leadership style called Authentic Leadership. I have expanded the research in this area related to this subject matter with a central premise that this style of leadership could play a major role in building authentic relationships. Authentic Leadership had emerged as a response to a call for a higher standard of character and integrity. Since 2003 when Avolio and Gardener introduced the term "authentic leadership," it had gained increased attention in the scholarly and practitioner communities. When formulating their theory of authentic leadership, Luthans and Avolio began with a discussion of how leaders at all levels and types of organizations are facing the challenge of moral decline and confidence in themselves and their associates. They believe that the kind of leadership that can restore confidence comes from individuals who are true to themselves, and whose transparency positively transforms or develop followers into leaders themselves.

Particularly with the rash of corporate and church, scandals that have awakened our collective consciousness to the fact that self-interest unchecked by moral reasoning and obligation can result in destructive behaviors. As I stated in the beginning and it is well worth emphasizing; these destructive behaviors not only destroy the lives of those who participate, but ultimately impacts thousands of innocent individuals as the outcomes trickle down, spilling over into the communities, and destroying families. Therefore, it is imperative that we directly examine the moral underpinnings to all modern professionals including medical doctors, lawyers, engineers, politicians, media professionals, ministers, professors, and everyday workers in any field, as we interface with them at one point or another.

Leaders who are *becoming* authentic in their style of leadership monitor their words and actions demonstrating they are aware of the negative or positive impact these actions can have on those they lead. However, to build on this point there needs to be a clear understanding that people who are becoming authentic are operating in the uppermost levels of integrity and morality. They do so to ensure they are building enduring relationships and institutions with the highest levels of credibility. In 2015 the *Harvard Business Review* declared "Authenticity has emerged as the gold standard for Leadership." The understanding is that these types of leaders are not without flaws, but they acknowledge their strengths and weaknesses and make a conscious effort to learn from their imperfections. By doing so, they acknowledge that this could be a lifelong process.

Luthans and Avolio have also identified several proactive positive characteristics that further define authentic leadership: "They operate from a set of end values that focus their behavior on doing what they perceive to be right for those they lead. Because they are value-centered, these leaders seek to reduce any existing gaps between their espoused values and their enacted values. This attempts to reduce any existing credibility gaps and requires authentic leaders to be aware of potential vulnerabilities and transparent enough to allow discussion of these areas with their followers. Authentic leaders also are willing to make the first move, taking the lead even when there is great risk in doing so. By doing so, these leaders model hopeful confidence in the future."[14]

Finally, authentic leaders have developed the capacity to examine moral dilemmas from several perspectives and make moral judgment calls when confronted with issues that do not have a clear solution." In line with the research of Luthans and Avolio's characteristics of authentic leaders, M. H. Kernis identified four basic characteristics of authentic leaders in an article from *Psychological Inquiry*: " self-awareness, unbiased processing of information, relational transparency, and authentic behavior—or behavior that is line with one's values, needs and preferences." To push this argument one step further Shamir and Eilam posit the following four characteristics of authentic leaders:

1. "Rather than faking their leadership, authentic leaders are true to themselves rather than conforming to the expectations of others.

2. Authentic leaders are motivated by personal convictions, rather than to attain status, honors, or other personal benefits.
3. Authentic leaders are originals, "not copies." That is, they lead from their own personal point of view.
4. The actions of authentic leaders are based on their personal values and convictions."[15]

Now it's your turn. In Table 5 below name four leaders that you consider to be authentic and why. This is strictly your opinion and remember being authentic does not mean you are perfect.

Table 5:

Name	Examples of their Authenticity

Choose Your Leadership Path

We all have positive and negative personality traits and are unique in our own right. Leadership styles can overlap as it is inevitable that leaders shift gears under pressure due to unexpected circumstances. Overall, my research provides a snapshot of the different leadership styles and it is up to each leader to define and fine-tune their style to achieve the stated mission and vision.

In summary, as we have seen, Charismatic leaders are often viewed as the head of the show, being larger than life, presenting themselves endowed with a special power. Transactional leaders' process is based on a mutual exchange to achieve a common goal. In addition, transformational leaders are diverse from charismatic and transactional leaders making them three distinct paradigms. Transformational leaders look for potential in their followers and seek to satisfy higher needs in their followers. The result of transformational leadership is a relationship of mutual stimulation that elevates the level of motivation and morality in both the leader and follower.

The research uncovered that Servant and Authentic leadership styles include a great deal of caring and concern for followers with respect to ensuring that the emphasis is on the *person*, not the product the person produces. In a Servant leadership style, people are valued, people are developed, and there is shared leadership. For Servant leaders, serving is not the means by which to get results, but the behavior of serving is the result.

Finally, the attributes of an authentic leader (one of the newest forms of leadership styles compared to the other styles) are being true to one's self and having a deep awareness of how a person thinks and behaves as well as how one is perceived by others. Authentic leaders admit to vulnerabilities and are transparent in their dealings with others. In other words, authentic leaders are relational.

I believe that effective leadership is born out of being relational, whereby the primary focus is not centered on the leader but how the leader interacts with their followers to build them into leaders. Authentic leadership is still in a developmental process. However, of all of the leadership styles, it is a provocative concept that holds promise toward *Raising The Bar*: **B**uilding **A**uthentic **R**elationships. As leaders, we must all choose to do better.

Chapter 2: Leadership Styles

Authentic Check-up

1. From the five leadership styles in this chapter, which one do you identify with the most and why?

____

____

____

____

2. Which leadership style(s) have you encountered the most in your career? How were you able to operate within that style?

____

____

____

____

3. Do you prefer to work with a team that has a similar leadership style to yours or another style that compliments yours?

____

____

____

____

4. Which authentic leader's qualities resonate with you most? i) self-awareness; ii) unbiased; iii) transparent; and iv) moral values. Choose two and explain.

5. Do you think inauthentic behavior is prevalent in the church and the workplace environment? If yes, describe. If no, explain.

CHAPTER 3

WOMEN IN LEADERSHIP

"Because I am a woman, I must make unusual efforts to succeed. If I fail, no one will say, "She doesn't have what it takes." They will say, "Women don't have what it takes."
— Clare Boothe Luce

The "Sheroes" need to be recognized. Among the many questions that are often at the center of deliberation are whether leadership is innate and whether women can lead. The first question has been debated in many circles. It's not surprising that some say "leaders are born" and you can't be taught to be a great leader. Other thought leaders argue that it is definitely possible to learn leadership skills with the right motivation and guidance. There is a great deal of research to support the theory that with the right training and experience, anyone can become a great leader.

Regarding the second question, I am perfectly clear on the answer— women can lead and are leading at exceptional levels. Leadership should not be a question of gender, but one of skill sets, capabilities, and experience. Studies have shown that top corporate female executives exhibit the same leadership behaviors as their male counterparts.[16] In addition, a Catalyst study of followers on comparing male to female leaders revealed common stereotypes like women were more nurturing, empathetic and responded in a timely fashion. Yet participants did say the women leaders they followed were a bit moody. The male leaders, on the other hand, were viewed by the survey participants as being more "action-oriented and focused."[17] Let's face it, men and women are different in many ways, but stepping up to the plate and leading a cause bigger than yourself that you are passionate about, has no gender built into the title.

There are a few references to women's leadership in the Bible compared to men, yet when women are mentioned in a leadership capacity, it is very significant. As a female leader, it is my obligation to briefly discuss the dynamics of women leading and the incredible contributions women are making in the church, workplace and on the world's largest stages.

From a Biblical perspective, the larger debate is should women be allowed to lead? Within many churches, gender-based discrimination has been reinforced by theological perspectives. The case that women are forbidden to lead by interpretation of Scripture and church tradition has been made for centuries. This exclusion is based predominantly on two Pauline texts:1 Timothy 2:11-15, and 1 Corinthians 14:33-34.

"Let a woman learn in silence with all submission. And I do not permit a woman to teach or to have authority over a man, but to be in silence. For Adam was formed first, then Eve. And Adam was not deceived, but the woman being deceived, fell into transgression. Nevertheless she will be saved in childbearing if they continue in faith, love, and holiness, with self-control." (1 Timothy 2:11-15).

"For God is not *the author* of confusion but of peace, as in all the churches of the saints. Let your women keep silent in the churches, for they are not permitted to speak; but *they are* to be submissive, as the law also says." (1 Corinthians 14:33-34).

In Paul's letter to Timothy, he was addressing the main problem that Timothy faced in the church of Ephesus—false prophets. Although, Paul specifically addresses women in this passage, there is a centuries old debate as to whether he meant women could not or should not learn the teachings. Likewise, in Paul's letter to the Corinthian church he wrote a similar comment to clarify what he believed to be the erroneous views of the church leaders and reiterated that women are to be silent in the churches and take a subordinate place under the Law.[18] I am in favor of a broader position that sees men and women as being ontologically equal but functionally different.

In her book, *Not Without A Struggle: Leadership Development for African American Women in Ministry,* Bishop Vashti M. McKenzie shares, "Some African-American male ministers have no problem rejecting Paul's command to slaves to be obedient to their masters as valid justification to outlaw slavery, but they close the door to women with their stance regarding Paul's comments about women being silent in the church and teaching. [19]

Further, Dr. Estrelda Alexander President of Seymour College, in her book, *Philip's Daughters: Women in Pentecostal-Charismatic Leadership* notes:

> "The Baptist womb for which the Church of God (COG) emerges gave the movement an early model for ministry with a clear conviction that the New Testament is the basis for all decisions and a tendency toward eliminating women in ministry. Typical Baptist congregations would grant a license to preach to qualify men who testified of a call to ministry. They would then ordain those who were called by the local congregation to serve as pastors or other specific ministry such as the deacons. Due to their interpretation

> of biblical passages related to women and ministry most Baptist did not recognize women as preachers or pastors. This was not universally exclusive, however, in the independence of each Baptist congregation allow for some variation. [20]

I know there are mixed feelings being in a church that traditionally did not have women leaders. I served in church as a full-time Assistant to the Pastor in an ordained pastoral role. As destiny would have it, the senior pastor of the church was dismissed from the local clergy conference the day of my ordination. While I rejoiced in that church service knowing this was a pivotal point in my journey, I also knew that there would be clouds over my head. I had to be strong as I was entering a world where there would be opposition from a significant population of men and women who felt I was stepping out of my lane after earning the title, "Woman Preacher."

That was over 25 years ago and the reality is that this opposition still exists in many churches today and in the workplace. Yet, women are tirelessly working to break the so- called glass ceiling. Since we tend to go above and beyond whatever we are challenged to do, we are recycling those glass pieces into successful leadership roles in publicly traded companies in technology, finance and medicine. We are no longer hiding in the shadows and have taken center stage in countless male-dominated professions despite the resistance. While there have been many stories of women climbing the success ladder to achieve their goals in the church and workplace, there are still far too many women that continue to fight the battles for recognition as a legitimate leader. Personally I don't believe there is a single formula for making women more effective as leaders. However, if leadership is to be a transformative vessel, there must be a relational component displayed when the leaders interact with her followers. Being a leader is about relationships whether you are a male or female.

In the church and beyond, on the national and international scene, women like; Michelle Obama, Nancy Pelosi, Madeleine Albright, Janet Yellen, Sheryl Sandberg, Ambassador Suzan Johnson Cook, Carla Harris, Valerie Jarrett, Kelly Brown Douglas, Co-Pastor Susie Owens, and Congresswoman Eleanor Holmes Norton, are just a handful of superb examples of outstanding women leadership. They are not imitations of men or other women who have come before them. They are originals operating in their unique and authentic giftings.

Global Leadership

As churches and businesses are expanding their reach in all parts of the world there appears to be a lack of experienced global leaders. Since it is well established that leadership is a complex subject, it would benefit all leaders to have a global perspective in operations as well as an understanding of the cultural differences. Today's leaders cannot ignore cultural differences in global markets, as it could be a sure sign of impending failure. Gone are the days of relying on old skill sets in managing relationships with global workforces. My research demonstrated that for leaders to meet the challenge of being a global leader, they must be equipped with a high level of Global Intelligence, or "GQ"—not the magazine.

GQ requires leaders to have the capability and flexibility to adapt to a changing world expeditiously. They must be self-aware in knowing their strengths and weaknesses. It demands a level of unpretentiousness where the leader has the foresight to recognize that other cultures may have an improved way of operating that are rooted in their cultural customs. This is not always easy to do when so many American leaders are entrenched in the Western culture and are comfortable or stuck in their way of doing things. Curiosity and desire should play a role in a global leaders' success, and they must be willing to learn about the cultural differences in person, and not just from the Cliff Notes or second-hand. The saying, "Walk a mile in my shoes" as first expressed by Cherokee Indians, sheds light on the actions that American leaders need to take abroad. Global leaders must show empathy in their adeptness to walk in the shoes of leaders of different cultures. They must be willing to venture out from their ivory towers and eat, sit and live amongst leaders of different cultures.

Alignment has become a gold standard of exceptional leadership. To align cultural differences is to acknowledge the values and commitments of each group with respect and dignity. Collaboration and integration are key ways global leaders can engage other leaders across mutual objectives while benefiting from the skill sets of those who make up the group. Finding ways to integrate local concerns with corporate concerns is not an easy task and may call for a more complex strategy. However, in doing so, it will enhance the global organization's viable competitive edge in engaging both markets.

In Bill George's article, *People + Strategy: The New Global Leaders,* George's assertion speaks to the need for inclusiveness that is evident in authentic relationships. Years ago, executives in both American and foreign companies were run by nationals. Even the former CEO of Siemens, Peter Loescher an Austrian, once said,

"... at Japanese, Indian, Chinese, and German companies it is rare that a non-national executive breaks into the company's top ranks. Siemens is not achieving its full potential on the international stage because its management is too white, too German, and too male. If you don't reflect your global client base, you cannot achieve your full potential."

There is no getting around the fact that we are becoming more globally connected through people, products, and technology. It is important that we all commit to broadening our understanding of different cultures, languages, and customs in order to better carry out the vision and goals of our companies. Just like we go to the doctor for checkups, leaders and team members should make it a priority to have yearly GQ checkups, in a learning and team-building environment. Step out of your comfort zone for a moment. Don't just walk in the shoes of someone from a different culture—run in them!

Global Female Leadership

Women have fought for a voice and representation in boardrooms and politics for years. Despite the obstacles, there are several powerful women running large successful organizations around the world. More important, although we have yet to witness a female president of the United States, many countries have had countless women leaders serve with effectiveness and integrity. America needs to embrace a new shift for female Commander in Chief. Today, there are a number of great women leaders in the following countries:

Helle Thorning-Schmidt, Prime Minister of Denmark

Yingluck Shinawatra, Prime Minister of Thailand

Angela Merkel, Chancellor of Germany

Cristina Fernández de Kirchner, President of Argentina

Dilma Rousseff, President of Brazil

Julia Gillard, Prime Minister of Australia

Ellen Johnson Sirleaf, President of Liberia

Sheik Hasina Wajed, Prime Minister of Bangladesh

Over the past few years, significant changes in leadership diversity in national and international global markets for women leadership have increased as of 2018. See Table 6.

Table 6:

Name	Occupation	Country/ Origin	Achievement
Indra Nooyi	Former Chairwoman, CEO PepsiCo Company	Indian American	Company's net profit since she started 6.5 billions dollars.
Roya Mahboo	CEO/President Afghan Citadel Software Company and Founder of the Digital Citizen Fund	USA/ Afghanistan	Named in TIME Magazine's 100 most influential people in the world for work in building internet classrooms in schools in Afghanistan and bridging the divide in technology for women and children in developing countries.
Alissa Abdullah, PhD	VP, Chief Information Security Officer Xerox	USA/African American	She established and currently leads, a corporate-wide information risk management program.

Name	Occupation	Country/ Origin	Achievement
Xiao Xue	Designer, Publisher & Editorial Director of ELLE China Magazine	China/ Chinese	No.1 in fashion media platform in China
Maidie Arkutu	Vice President Unilever Francophone	Ivory Coast, West Africa	Honored by the Business Excellence magazine for most outstanding Manufacturing Executive Personal Products at the 2nd Feminine Ghana Achievement Awards 2016.
Kristine Braden	Chief of Staff to Citigroup CEO	Switzerland/ American	In 2017, she was appointed to the board of Swiss Banking association, the first female board member in the association's history. The Bank manages 26.6 billion. Making it one of the larger foreign firms in Switzerland.

Name	Occupation	Country/ Origin	Achievement
Dr. Amy Jadesimi	CEO of Lagos Deep Offshore Logistics (LADOL) a private owned company	Nigeria	Nigerian physician, businesswoman, entrepreneur and Corporate Officer. CEO of a 500 million Industrial Free Zone. In 2014 Forbes named her among the 20 Youngest Power Women in Africa
Cathy Hughes	Founder Radio One	American	Entrepreneur, television and radio personality and business executive who has a network of $460 million.
Mellody Hobson	President & Co-CEO of Ariel Investments in Chicago.	American	Manages over 13 billion in assets. Will become Vice Chair at Starbucks when Howard Schultz steps down in July 2018. A company with a global market.

The successful women leaders in the chart do not scratch the surface of the accomplishments of women leaders across the globe from large corporations to solopreneurs. Many of the favorable attributes of great leadership are innate qualities that women already have, including empathy, nurturing, attentive listener, team approach, multitasking, and the ability to balance home and work, are just a few examples.

Yet despite all of the strides that women have made in the workplace, there is still a gender pay gap that continues to rear its head. Women make 77.9 cents per every dollar that men earn[21]. In addition, research shows that women and men start out making the same amount of money early in their careers but then men are given more career opportunities so they end up earning considerably more. Therefore, a lot more work needs to be done in ensuring that women have equal opportunities to advance their careers.

Great leaders are needed in all facets of society. Whether in the church, in the workplace, local, national or international levels, you can't escape or negate the need for genuine, authentic leadership. The reality is that without healthy, positive, and effective leadership, churches and organizations will not grow into their full potential which will more than likely create large debt for the organizations, while leaving individuals stagnant, worried, and unfulfilled.

Now that we have established how the characteristics of a leader's capacity and influence play in achieving greater results, we need to shift our focus not so much on what leaders say, but what they do and how they do it. Therefore, we will explore some of the recognized leadership styles to determine which ones are helping or hurting to build authentic relationships.

Chapter 3: Women in Leadership

Authentic Check-up

1. Do you believe women can be effective leaders? If yes explain. If not explain.

2. Why do you think there is so much opposition to women in leadership?

3. Name your favorite woman leader. Why?

4. Have you ever had a woman as your boss? Share in one or two sentences what stood out to you about her leadership style?

____

____

____

____

5. How was she different from your male boss?

____

____

____

____

PART II

Be True to Yourself

"I'm spending more time promoting myself than I am being myself."

CHAPTER 4

WILL THE REAL YOU PLEASE STAND UP!

Defining Authentic Leadership

For a long time, I could not define what causes a leader to talk one way in public and then walk an entirely different way in their private space. I knew there was something wrong, but this diametrical behavior was difficult for me to explain. How could a person use sound judgment in making decisions, treat their team fairly and with respect in meetings and across the pulpit, yet that same person steal from the organization, abuses minors, or engages in other criminal activity? I realized that this type of double-faced behavior was the result of leaders lacking authenticity and constant rationalization that it is OK to lie (even just a little white lie) to get ahead.

The truth of the matter is that cheating, lying or even stealing to get ahead may appear beneficial in the beginning, but in the long run, you will lose much more than you gained. Leaders fail to realize that every person connected to that leader is negatively impacted by the inauthentic relationship that has been brought to light. Many of these relationships are downright toxic, leaving little room for authentic behavior to be displayed.

When it comes to any discussion of authentic or inauthentic behavior amongst leaders, the lines have become blurred. Some leaders in the church are couching their unscrupulous behavior under the guise of "doing the work of God to expand the Kingdom." Yet, just beneath the surface, these leaders are concerned with gaining "rock-star" status and increasing their personal wealth to acquire more "toys." On the other side, leaders in the workplace are more focused on the bottom line; placing products over people or getting a high return on their investments at any cost. In both instances, these leaders value "self" rather than "service." Power over people and greed has taken center stage in their lives. Unfortunately, far too many leaders have been seduced into believing that the criterion for success is all about power, prestige, and money. When these selfish pursuits are unchecked, these leaders find themselves on a collision course for destruction.

Although the concept of authenticity is not new, there is a resurgence of attention being paid to what constitutes authentic, inauthentic, and pseudo behavior. Increasingly, leaders in the church and workplace are realizing the need for a greater level of accountability in their professional relationships. Especially since hypocrisy in the church and the workplace amongst leaders appears to be escalating daily. The need for an alternative paradigm is gaining momentum as followers and team members are lending their voices for a higher standard of behavior: spiritually, morally, and emotionally. What is not commonly seen in too many of these organizations is the vast relational disconnect between leaders and followers, which frequently causes a growing frustration and a decrease in the maximum productivity.

As you know, we are inundated with countless newspaper and magazine articles, websites, and blogs of the unethical behaviors and moral failures of leaders in the political arena, small and large corporations, as well as churches. Leaders in all denominations are being exposed. Whether it is the Catholic Church sexual abuse cases, Protestant, Baptist, Methodist, and Evangelical Church leaders' infidelity, financial scandals, and other illegal activity, is front and center in the media. The sensationalized headlines by news outlets such as *The New York Times*, *Wall Street Journal*, and *The Washington Post*, saturate our news feeds and social media on a regular basis.

In this age of technology, exposure to such behavior is at the touch of a button. With Instagram, Twitter, YouTube, Facebook, and other social media outlets, very little is hidden from the public view. Notwithstanding, these unethical behaviors are costing our economy billions of dollars as many of these disputes are settled through our court systems.

For leaders who are trying to raise the bar and live authentic lives, despair is real because it seems everywhere you turn, a highly esteemed leader falls. Despite the increased negative attention and activity, I strongly believe that there are far more leaders in the church and workplace that are determined to live authentic lives than their inauthentic counterparts in the spotlight. Over the last 30 years, I have been on this journey with the privilege of serving with leaders in government, private sector, and on full-time staff for four churches; two were considered megachurches. During these years, I observed hundreds of leaders exemplifying the various leadership styles. Although I may not have agreed with all of their decision-making, I can say that none of them have been in the spotlight for inauthentic behaviors.

Unfortunately, on the flip side of the coin, I have also witnessed the good, the bad, and the ugly in how some leaders and followers form and maintain relationships. Yes, the majority of these that I have served and observed, operate from a high bar, valuing and respecting their teams. Yet, there are far too many leaders who operate from a place where the bar is low. There is very little sense of camaraderie and fairness. Deception and disputes creep into the environment and are on full display then this culture becomes the norm. Individuals are sabotaged because of jealousy and self-interests so that the flavor of the month can flourish and push their one-sided agenda. In a nutshell, leaders have been blindsided in allowing inauthentic behavior to claim the main stage, overshadowing a culture of honor and integrity.

What does it mean to be Authentic?

The concept of being authentic is often misunderstood. The reality is that there are no cookie-cutter approaches to becoming authentic. The truth is, being authentic is not trying to emulate someone else. Authentic behavior is developed when individuals live out their unique story, understanding who they are, where they came from and where they are going. No two people have identical DNA, life story or life experiences. Therefore, trying to emulate another person will ultimately result in one person being an imposter. To be precise, authentic leaders are "originals" who lead from their own personal points of convictions.

Authenticity has been defined in many ways. Webster's dictionary defines "authentic" as being "real, genuine, trustworthy, and reliable." While the Oxford English dictionary states authenticity is "undisputed origin." The word originally comes from the Greek word Authetntikos, meaning 'principal or genuine." With the Oxford definition, we may be putting people and more importantly leaders, under the same level of scrutiny as we might consider a rare piece of jewelry. Being authentic is a matter of the absence of any intention to deceive at any level. In pop culture, authenticity to generation X, Z and the Millennials, coined the term, "Keep it 10o". In short, one's inside matches one's outside actions.

Defining authenticity is a subject matter that is often difficult to characterize as individuals connect with each other. It's a term that you know it when you see it, but sometimes it's hard to label. Being authentic is a very awkward thought to spell out and often even tougher to live out. It is risky, scary, nor is it easy or convenient. It will often require you to be vulnerable and courageous at the same time. It's also more than just being honest and trustworthy.

Researchers Bruce Avolio and Frank Luthans studied authentic individuals and found, "these individuals are confident, hopeful, optimistic, resilient and of high moral character." [22] To build on this point, Avolio and Luthans identified positive characteristics that define authentic leadership concluding: "they operate from a set of end values that focus their behavior on doing what they perceive to be right for themselves and those they lead. Because they are value-centered individuals. These leaders seek to reduce any existing gaps between their espoused values and their enacted values."[23]

This attempt to reduce any credibility gaps requires authentic leaders to be aware of potential vulnerabilities, blind spots, and be transparent enough to allow discussion of these areas with their team. Authentic leaders are also willing to make the first move, taking the lead even when there are great risks. Authentic leaders have developed the capacity to examine moral dilemmas from several perspectives and make moral judgment calls when confronted with issues that do not have a clear solution. [24]

Scholars, Michael Kernis and Brian Goldman, have weighed in by defining this abstract concept and agree that being authentic is "the unimpeded operations of one's true or core self in one's daily enterprises." In line with Luthans and Avolio's characteristics of authentic leadership, Kernis identified four basic characteristics of an authentic leader in an article, entitled *Psychological Inquiry,* where he specifies the four basic dimensions of authenticity are: Self-awareness, Unbiased processing of information, Relational transparency, Authentic behavior—or behavior that is line with one's values, needs, and preferences. [25]

In layman's terms, the journey to becoming authentic is a unique undertaking for each person, since each one of us is on a different personal journey. It's about how you chose to navigate your journey. We are not all dealt the same hand in life. Yet it is our responsibility to turn our hand into a winning hand, despite the obstacles that may come into play.

The reality is in every leader's life there will be joys and sorrows. However, too often there are more disappointments, detours, and distractions that hinder our journey. Like the line from the movie *Forrest Gump*, "life is like a box of chocolate; you never know what you are going to get." Nonetheless, even though you have no idea what you are going to be faced with, yet the one thing that you do know is that you are dealing with human beings with emotions, challenges, experiences, highs, and lows. And just like Forrest kept running, you as the leader must keep running your own race. You must endeavor each day to define what being authentic means to you as you handle the vicissitudes of your personal life and the lives of those you lead.

Let the Journey Begin

Now that the need for authenticity and what it means to be authentic has been examined, it's time to revisit that path to becoming authentic from several practical angles, asking more thought-provoking questions. Is authenticity the road less travel by leaders? Are there leaders who are truly living authentic lives? If so how did they get there? These are the questions that I have asked myself as I journey to become authentic. I believe many other leaders have asked these same questions.

While I will acknowledge becoming an authentic leader is a lofty ambition in the relational progress, it is by no means a cakewalk. Unfortunately, there is not an Authenticity App that you can download to check-in. Think about what specific action steps need to be mapped out for leaders to become authentic and build authentic relationships? How will leaders know when they have arrived at that place where others can rightfully call them an authentic leader?

There is ample data from many decades in organizational performance that becoming authentic is a learned behavior. Not necessarily from textbooks, seminars, or 10-step programs. No, it is the leader's ability to step out of their comfort zone and lead with an internal compass that helps them navigate through challenging situations and remain faithful to what they have learned about themselves and what they believe to make a difference in their world without any fear of repercussion. It is the authentic leader's solitary purpose to move to another level on a relational journey and shape their environment to elevate moral and ethical behavior.

Therefore, the journey to authenticity is fostered by the way leaders live their lives in the broader society; publicly and privately. They must align their positive values and beliefs to restore confidence in leadership and respond to demands for a greater level of accountability within their organizations. As a result, constructive and enduring outcomes can be advanced by leaders, especially when the leader is mindful of the fact that this does not happen overnight. For many leaders, it could be a life-long journey. However, in the end, the benefits are worth every struggle along the way.

For a leader to be authentic they must realize the journey is more important than the destination. Understanding that "being" is not as important as "becoming." The leader must decide, "Do I want to be," or "Do I want to become." In "becoming" it is about the process and the rewards. John Ruskin, a prominent social thinker and philanthropist stated, "the highest reward for a person's toil is not what they get for it, but what they become by it." Authentic leaders are more concerned about helping their followers move from being to becoming. The Bible teaches us that we are a work in progress. In Philippians 1:6, 'Being confident of this very thing, that He who has begun a good work in you will complete it until the day of Jesus Christ."

After self-examination of my own leadership style and recollecting several painful struggles and mistakes in handled prior relationships, I discovered that there were periods of time when I was not operating as an authentic leader. Many times I would have my colleagues say, "You carry yourself as if nothing bothers you." Deep down inside I knew that was not true. I had major insecurities that I placed on myself and would not open that door and share with others. I preferred to wear the mask, pretending I had it all together. All the time walking around like I had an "S" on my chest and screaming on the inside for someone to help me.

I felt a sense of insignificance in my roles, even though my title spoke the opposite. My feelings of insignificance caused me to be angry and annoyed when those around me claimed their fame. Since I did not feel worthy, why should they, was my frame of reference. These feelings also lead me to not trust and value those in my sphere of influence without cause. Because I was miserable, the old saying became true, "misery loves company," and I wanted others to feel the same negative emotions that I felt. I did not deliberately try to hurt people, I just didn't do anything to enhance their times of celebration but wore a fake smile on my face.

I remember when I was in seminary, several years after being in the workforce, a classmate who I had rarely communicated with, said, "You need to tell your story." At first, I thought to myself, *what is she talking about and who was she to say that to me*? I knew exactly what she meant. I was not being true to who I was and was in fear of anyone finding out. After my pity party, I decided to own this truth. I had been guilty of wearing a disguise in many of my relationships and I needed to make a change because of my lack of authenticity.

In my desire to be transparent there were three incidents in my life that tried to keep me from becoming and growing into an authentic healthy leader:

1. Being a single parent always caused me a sense of strife and anxiety until I realized that God had brought forth a miracle in my daughter who has exceeded my expectations as a successful business owner and ordained minister.
2. I felt discarded by those who did not see my value. It caused me to feel insecure, lonely, and bitter until I realized that I could not spend my life operating by what other people thought of me. There was no reason to accept their views because God promised me that I had a great future ahead of me.
3. God allowed a major challenge to come my way that rocked my world— my very being. This attack was literally designed by the enemy to take me out, but at the end of the day, I learned that it was for my good. Romans 8:28 "And we know that all things work together for good to those who love God, to those who are called according to His purpose." The main lesson I learned

was that God was shaping character in me that may not have been built in any other way.

Healthy Leadership

"When the leader grows, everyone around the leader grows."

The health of any organization depends upon the health of its leadership. In his book, *Leading from the Inside Out- The Art of Self-Leadership*, Samuel D. Rima, profoundly states, "if a person can't effectively lead his own life and control [herself] how should [she] be expected to provide effective leadership to others?" Now, I don't want to come off as trying to psychoanalyze the situation, but Rima reminds us that if we don't have our act together in our own homes, how can we expect to be effective in running things outside of our homes.

Healthy leadership is about the positive influence that produces positive outcomes. At the heart of the matter, leadership is not about a title, a position or having a corner office with a window. It is about how leaders use their influence to add value to those they lead. Simon Sinek said in an interview with SUCCESS Magazine, "Leadership is not about being in charge, it is about taking care of those in your charge." [26] Healthy leaders not only motivate leaders in their sphere of influence, but they also empower leaders to become better leaders. When there is a lack of healthy leadership, everyone around suffers and there is a decline in productivity and morality in some form or another in the church and in the workplace.

People value the person who will stand up and take charge and get things done with moral integrity. It is the leaders who inspire those who accept the challenge and accomplish things beyond their wildest dreams. When a healthy leader steps up to the plate, transformation takes place. That transformation produces people emboldened to take action to create a climate where business, as usual, is not the norm from the highest to lowest levels of the organization.

Healthy leadership is the underpinning of all of the accomplishments in our families, churches, communities, organizations, and corporations. Therefore, having a concise understanding of the concept of healthy leadership deserves the utmost attention in discovering the leader's best practices on how she operates to steward success in reaching and exceeding objectives. Every church and workplace craves for strong healthy leadership, so it is important to lead in P.E.A.C.E.

Go in P.E.A.C.E

How do leaders who are *becoming* authentic use their influence in relationships? To answer this question, it is important to understand that authentic relationships must start from healthy leadership. Any leader who desires to *become* authentic and is not healthy starts off with a major deficit and is pushing uphill. My observation has been that there is a thin line between healthy and unhealthy behavior amongst those in leadership positions. Leadership is an extraordinary vocation, it comes with great demands, yet not always with substantial remuneration. At a minimum, authentic leaders should promote **P.E.A.C.E** and reduce stress and anxiety within their organizations. I define healthy leadership as:

- **Positive:** Support and respect team members is a foundation for the leader to build upon.
- **Effective:** Visible change is seen in the leader's behavior first, and then within the team.
- **Available:** Leaders engage their team by giving them access through an open-door policy that doesn't intrude upon the leaders' productivity.

- **Creative:** Leaders create a safe space for expression, thinking outside of the box, and encourage team members to do the same.
- **Empowering:** The leader creates a supportive atmosphere that allows followers to step up and lead by working independently and making decisions.

Chapter 4: Will The Real You Please Stand!

Authentic Check-up

1. In one sentence what does being authentic mean to you?

2. Doe your private behavior match your public behavior? If yes, share one or two brief thoughts that demonstrate this. If no, what areas do you need to improve upon?

3. What qualities do you attribute to a person you feel is authentic? Name at least two.

4. When a person is inauthentic, what effect do you think they have in their organizations?

____

____

____

____

5. How can authentic leaders help leaders who are exhibiting inauthentic behavior?

____

____

____

____

PART III

Self Evaluation

"I would like you to be more self-reliant, show more initiative, and take greater personal responsibility — but check with me first!"

CHAPTER 5

PERSONAL LEADERSHIP DEVELOPMENT

Self Evaluation

> *"To thine own self be true, and it must follow, as the night the day, thou canst not then be false to any man."*
> — ***William Shakespeare***

As a leader, the sooner you embrace the thought that leadership is not a stagnant way of being, the better your chances of success. One of your primary leadership goals should be to always seek to improve and grow at every stage of your career. Staying abreast of your strengths, weaknesses, and leadership style will help you become a more effective leader. Therefore, as you are striving to become authentic, begin to both conceptualize and visualize that your development and growth is a lifetime course of action. The reality is, no leader has finally arrived.

Since we are all human, our actions are often based upon our circumstances. Is it a routine occurrence? Is it a crisis? Is there a middle ground position? Leaders tend to fluctuate between being authentic and inauthentic based upon the gravity of the situation. With that in mind, every leader needs to take personal responsibility to enhance and maintain their abilities and knowledge as they lead. As stated previously, all leaders must be on an intentional journey of continuous improvement, which can't happen without human intervention, in the areas of specific development and growth.

Personal Leadership Development Growth Plan (PLDGP)

Authentic leaders must be actively involved in their ongoing *Personal Leadership Developmental Growth Plan* (PLDGP). Since you are always in a developmental mode to think and rethink your relationship-building skill sets. Specifically, what have you learned and accomplished, and how to build upon your skill sets for the future, to further impact lives in your organizations. A typical PLDGP plan should include your vision for your future as well as S.M.A.R.T Goals (Specific, Measurable, Attainable, Results-Driven, and Timely.

When leaders are involved in a PLDGP, whether it's formal or informal, they can assess how they've handled relationships in the past and utilize new metrics to improve their interactions in the future. The key is maintaining old relationships and building new ones. A PLDGP is also a vehicle for leaders to honestly evaluate and reflect on their strengths and weaknesses. It is the leader's readiness to maintain a PLDGP that will enhance the leader's ability to move to another level of development and growth, in order to build authentic relationships with those in their sphere of influence. If leaders are not developing and growing, then more than likely their followers will not be developing and growing, which leads to high turnover and ultimately expenses.

Often, when it comes to the development and growth plan, too many leaders put the focus on their followers and never look in the mirror to see how they are measuring up. Leaders must be careful that they don't become prideful like the Emperor in Hans Christian Anderson's famous tale, "The Emperor's New Clothes." Despite the fact that everyone could see that the Emperor was naked, the townspeople were afraid to speak up, until a child cried out, "But he isn't wearing any clothes!" This tale also demonstrates the concepts of collective denial and honesty as a virtue. No one wanted to speak the truth to an authority figure for fear of becoming a target for repercussions or being out of step with the majority. We must approach certain critical situations with child-like honesty.

Know Thyself

Knowing thyself is a pre-qualifier for authentic behavior.

Self-examination is essential for developing and growing leaders. Whether anyone speaks the truth to leaders or not, all leaders must be guided by an inner voice of self-awareness and self-management. They should have a gut feeling that says, *something is not quite right and I need to make a few changes.* With no self-examination plan, leaders and their followers could be in for embarrassing moments.

I believe there are three critical elements in the self-examination process that leaders can benefit from as they strive to become authentic. These elements are factors in their developmental growth continuum, and not necessarily in order:

- Knowing one's self/ yourself;
- Being true to yourself; and
- Identifying/Defining Core Values.

Each element should be addressed separately. All too often in a development and growth plan, people try to complete these factors all at the same time. This could lead to feeling overwhelmed and giving up before a true assessment is created. For this reason, I want to remind you of the old adage, "How do you eat an elephant? One bite at a time!"

Step 1:

The first step towards becoming authentic in your PLDGP can be captured under the rubric, "To know one's self." In a functional sense, to know yourself means being comfortable in your own skin. It's owning your personal experiences through thoughts, emotions, and beliefs. "The reality is that you cannot do what you say if you do not know what you believe." Consider using self-awareness tools such as The Myers-Briggs Personality Assessment, the DISC Assessment Tool or Peer Assessment. Knowing yourself requires having conversations with yourself that invoke your true identity. It makes you more aware of what you want to do and gives you the reasons why you want to do it. These important conversations will help you find your distinctive voice and your niche in the marketplace which will help you thrive in a less artificial way. Remember, it's OK to talk to yourself, as long as you don't answer back!

> Knowing oneself is the ability to clarify one's values and beliefs that will guide one's actions.

Knowing yourself can be the benchmark in discerning whether a leader can and cannot compromise as it relates to their decisions. Making decisions is less encumbered with each scenario when a leader knows himself or herself. When leaders say, "yes or no" they can do so without hesitation or feelings of guilt.

Being authentic means that the leader's choices are based on personal courage and moral convictions. It was Eleanor Roosevelt who said, "One's philosophy is not best expressed in words, it is expressed in the choices one makes." Authentic leaders are motivated by their convictions, rather than opportunities to attain status, honor or other personal benefits.

In *The Gifts of Imperfections,* Brene' Brown makes the case for "being authentic," when she states, "authenticity is a collection of choices to show up and be real. The choice to be honest and the choice to let our true selves be seen. [27] So, the question comes down to how can a person be authentic if they do not know and comprehend themselves?

Part of the challenge for leaders who are attempting to live authentic lives is that much of our society is focused on the external. In turn, being authentic is more focused on an inward journey. Howard Thurman an influential African American author, theologian, and educator stated in his book *The Inward Journey,* "There is something in every one of you that waits and listens for the sound of the genuine in yourself. It is the only true guide you will ever have. And if you cannot hear it, you will all of your life spend your days on the ends of strings that somebody else pulls." [28] As we see in Scripture, "My sheep know my voice and another they will not follow."[29]

Focusing inwardly can be challenging for many leaders because in today's instant social media environment, everything is staged. We are witnessing fictional lives and characters. Especially when a myriad of leaders show up on Facebook and Instagram with doctored photos, misleading profiles, and communicate to us on Twitter in two hundred and eighty characters or less, revealing only their best or false side. Authentic leaders do not need external approval from the masses to have internal satisfaction about their actions.

This journey is more about a leader's willingness to accept the challenge to discover their real self, which is one of the hardest jobs any leader will ever take on. Why? Because all of us are multifaceted, complex individuals with many real-world experiences. The greater understanding a leader has of himself or herself, the better they can make sense of the world they live in and how their understanding of the world may differ from others. A world where there are constant change and uncertainty.

Knowing who you are is acknowledging your strengths and weaknesses. In a sense, praying the prayer of Reinhold Niebuhr; "God grant me the serenity to accept the things I cannot change, courage to change the things I can, and the wisdom to know the difference" is one to add to your memory bank. Authentic leaders must acknowledge their inner selves before they deal with the outside environment, and admit "It's an Inside Job."

Be True to Yourself

"I prefer to be true to myself, even at the hazard of incurring the ridicule of others, rather than to be false and to incur my own abhorrence."
— Frederick Douglas

Step 2

To further the discussion on the elements for a *Personal Leadership Development Growth Plan* (PLDGP) the question that is often raised is, "What does being true to yourself really mean?" I believe being true to yourself means that you are completely honest with your feelings, and how you communicate those feelings to yourself and others. It means being courageous in expressing your truth and not worrying what others think of you. When you are true to yourself, it says that you know who you are, and you accept your good qualities, and are aware of your not so desirable qualities.

"It takes courage to grow up and become who you really are."

— E.E. Cummings

Being true to yourself opens the lines of communication and gives you the opportunity to receive feedback and listen to others, but at the end of the day, leaders need to make up their minds and not be swayed by the opinions of others to gain favor. When a leader stands up for what he believes and respects himself, he gains respect from others. The truth of the matter is, people can tell how you respect yourself by how you treat yourself. Do you take responsibility for your decisions? Do you forgive yourself when you make a mistake or error in judgment? Do you say "no" and stand by it? Your team, in turn, will follow suit in the example you set before them. The old adage is still true, "people will treat you the way you let them treat you." Leaders who are true to themselves learn to take responsibility for their lives.

However, being your "true self" does not give you a license to be callous and insensitive to the feelings and voices of others. While being your "true self" can take on a meaning that you are spontaneous, it does not mean that during your spontaneity, you are rude and disrespectful. On the other hand, to live an authentic life does not mean you are dormant. Being authentic has an ethical component as well as a practical side. With authentic behavior, there is always an element to proceed with an attitude of mutual respect regardless of where others fall in the hierarchy.

Some leaders blame their behavior on their personality or temperament. Again, this is not acceptable because leaders must have self-control. Being brutally honest with no filters does not make you authentic; instead, it makes you narcissistic. The phrase "what you see is what you get," is not acceptable amongst authentic leaders. Leaders can choose to express their true feelings, but they can also use sound judgment and choose not to if it means hurting someone. Yet they will remain authentic by having a high standard of character. Mutual respect is a principle of authenticity that will help leaders be more effective in their communications.

Another point on being authentic is that leaders must be careful not to become like windowpanes where people can see straight through them. Therefore, authentic leaders do not have to bare it all, and share every defeat, every failing and every struggle without discretion. There are times when leaders should remain silent because it is not the right time or place.

In Williams Shakespeare's "Hamlet," Polonius counseled his son Laertes—"to thine own self be true!" Although this line was spoken in the play in the early 1600s, it still holds true today. This same Shakespearean line was also spoken by Tupac Shakur's character in the movie, *All Eyez on Me.* Being true to yourself is one of the foundational pillars in *Raising the BAR: Building Authentic Relationships.* We must all make a conscious effort to be honest with ourselves and in our relationships in order to be authentic and live without regrets.

Keep in mind that being authentic is never about convenience. When someone says that the leader is authentic, one of the things they are really saying is that the leader's outward behavior is unwavering in what they say and do. Often this behavior comes from a set of Core Values, that embody deeply held beliefs.

Core Values

"Be yourself, everyone else is taken."

— Oscar Wilde

Step 3:

A leader's Core Values are traits that represent the essence of who the leader is as a human being. In other words, these values are what they stand for in whatever environment they find themselves. They are the central steering forces of a leader's beliefs and they set the leader's priorities. The leader's Core Values model the culture of the organization. Culture forms at the top. Why? Because the leader has a significant amount of power and authority, therefore his behavior sets the tone for what is expected and what is not in the organizational culture. When a leader clarifies his value system, that allows the leader to be held accountable to those in their sphere of influence. This is what can be summed up as Value-Based Leadership where everyone has value regardless of their organizational level. A deeper meaning of Core Values provides an easy to remember acronym to help leaders stay on track. This critical Personal Leadership Development piece will be further explored in the next chapter.

Chapter 5: Personal Leadership Development

Authentic Check-up

1. What steps are you taking to grow and develop in your personal and professional life? Name at least two. If the answer is none, why not? Create a plan to get started.

   ____

   ____

   ____

   ____

2. What does it mean to “Know One’s Self? Explain.

   ____

   ____

   ____

   ____

3. How have you handled honest feedback regarding your leadership in the past? If you responded negatively, what can you do differently? If positively, how has it helped in your personal growth?

   ____

   ____

   ____

   ____

4. In creating your PLDP, are you soliciting input from colleagues, team members, family members? How can this help your leadership in the future?

____

____

____

____

5. How many books, articles, do you read each month? Name two items you've read recently that impacted your leadership style or thought process.

____

____

____

____

CHAPTER 6

CORE VALUES: A KEY TO PERSONAL LEADERSHIP DEVELOPMENT, Cont.

Leaders must be mindful that followers mimic their actions consciously and unconsciously, in public and in private. Core values drives the leaders' decisions and define their purpose and mission, as they make sense of their view of the world. Leaders need to be aware that there is a difference between values and qualities. "Values are who you are, and qualities are what you do to honor your values" [30]according to Bob Rue, a Behavioral Scientist.

Every leader should have a set of positive core values that come from a mature, healthy, grounded place that will be a catalyst for transformation in the leader and their followers' lives. Matthew 6:21 makes the statement, "Where your treasure is, there your heart will be also." It is imperative that leaders have and operate on a set of core values and not just the ones that keep them in their comfort zone. Core values set the course on how leaders and followers interact with each other daily, and more so during times of crises, changes, and uncertainty. Your core values become strong pillars that can be used as guiding principles that enhance your ability to become authentic. Use your core values as filters to help keep you on a positive trajectory. Consider these terms below when you think of Core Values.

CORE VALUES SNAPSHOT

C= Consistent: Being authentic means your words are consistent with your "deeds," otherwise those you are in a relationship with will always see you as being disingenuous. It is true that leaders like all of us, may have a bad day, but we must be careful not to let those bad moments stretch out to a bad week or month.

O= Open-minded: Being open-minded ranks high on an authentic leader's list as they deal with day-to-day uncertainty. This allows the leader to be receptive to the views, ideas, and knowledge of their followers.

R= Reliable: In a simplistic way, a reliable leader is one you can count on to do what they say they will do. Being reliable is a vital part of the underpinning of any relationship and especially among authentic leaders and their followers.

E= Empathetic: One definition of the word "empathy" is the action of understanding, being aware of, being sensitive to and vicariously experiencing the feelings, thoughts, and experiences of another.

V= Vigilant: The definition of vigilant is the action or state of keeping a careful watch for possible danger or difficulties. This core value is not frequently heard in leadership circles today. Nonetheless, vigilance is one of the significant traits that leaders need to have themselves or the core member(s) of their team should exhibit this behavior.

A= Accountable: If a leader is not willing to wear the cloak of accountability, no matter how gifted or intelligent he is, failure and strife may be looming in the distance. Every leader should have accountability goals and objectives for themselves.

L= Life-Long Learner: Since we live in a world that is constantly changing, leaders must continue to expose themselves to knowledge. Whether it is in a formal or informal setting, personal and professional development should be a priority to remain relevant.

U= Understanding: When it comes to building relationships understanding can be paramount in whether there will be success or failure.

E= Ethical: The bottom line for ethical leaders is that they do the right thing for the right reason. Ethical leaders have within their core to be fearless to do what is right even if they are shunned by the majority.

S= Steward: God expects Believers to oversee all that He brings into their lives in a way that that it reverends God. Christians have come to recognize that they are only the steward and God is the owner.

"Success doesn't come from what you do occasionally.
It comes from what you do consistently."
— Marie Forleo

C= Consistent: Being authentic means your words are consistent with your "deeds," otherwise those you are in a relationship with will always see you as being disingenuous. It is true that leaders, may have a bad day, but we must be careful not to let those bad moments stretch out to a bad week or month. When Leaders are consistent in their behavior, they create an expectancy from their followers. For example, if a leader is always on time for meetings or events, others will show up on time because the leader has established the norm for start times. Just the opposite happens when a leader is inconsistent with their start times. Now, some followers may come on time, but there is a sense that their time is not valuable or their time is being wasted. Consistency is important and many leaders fail to realize that when they are not consistent, they send conflicting messages. When followers are uncertain of the leaders' behavior, it can lead to anxiety and lessen productivity. For this reason, leaders must be mindful to engage in consistent actions as part of their authentic growth—remember actions speak louder than words.

"It doesn't make sense to hire smart people and tell them what to do;
we hire smart people so they can tell us what to do."
— Steve Jobs

O= Open-minded: Being open-minded ranks high on an authentic leader's list as they deal with day-to-day uncertainty. This allows the leader to be receptive to the views, ideas, and knowledge of their followers. When leaders have an open mind, they can take their time to contemplate how to bring a resolution to a problem without jumping to quick conclusions. Open-minded leaders realize that they don't have to be the smartest person in the room. This is because they have the capacity to surround themselves with the brightness and best, those with more experience in areas where the leader is not the most proficient. This allows the leader to make decisions based on diverse creativity and innovation that could change the trajectory of the organization.

Authentic leaders understand that being open-minded helps to build confidence and self-esteem amongst followers, as opposed to followers feeling undervalued. When followers know that their voice is valued and heard they are prone to become more effective and efficient in carrying out their responsibilities. An authentic open-minded leader embraces new ideas from their followers, without partiality and politics, knowing it will also boost deeper relationships on the team. Open-minded leaders welcome the best ideas and are not concerned with who gets the credit, only that it is a win-win for the whole organization.

Now, the reality is that it can be difficult for some leaders to be open-minded because they have strong opinions and are reluctant to make a shift. The truth is a leader can have strong views and not be close-minded. Being open-minded does not mean the leader has to accept *all* new ideas, it means that the leader is willing to consider new ideas. When a leader's mind is closed or one-sided, it hinders the overall success of the organization and prevents collaboration and new ideas.

"There are those you can count and there are those you can count on."

— Anonymous

R= Reliable: In a simplistic way, a reliable leader is one you can count on to do what they say they will do. Being reliable is a vital part of the underpinning of any relationship and especially among authentic leaders and their followers. Dependable and reliable go together like a hand and glove. Merriam-Webster defines dependability as "Capable of being depended on; reliable." Reliable leaders are not only pledging their word to others but to themselves as well when they make a commitment to do something. Being a reliable leader means the leader doesn't over promise and under deliver.

If leaders are seeking to be reliable, they do so without excuses and blaming others. As soon as leaders know they can't fulfill the commitment, every effort must be made to let the person know of the changed circumstances. They bite the bullet and tell the truth without fudging it. By being truthful, the leader sets the bar high for followers to seek to achieve as well.

"Before you judge a man, walk a mile in his shoes."

— Mary T. Lathrap

E= Empathetic: One definition of the word "empathy" is the action of understanding, being aware of, being sensitive to and vicariously experiencing the feelings, thoughts, and experiences of another. Empathy is often confused with "sympathy" which falls in the category of feeling pity for someone concerning their situation. In layman's terms, empathy is the ability to place yourself in another person's shoes and see things from another person's perspective. Empathetic leaders have insight into why a person may be responding in a certain way. It is to try to feel what makes a person tick. Being an empathic leader builds stronger relationships.

Empathy has been called a right-brain activity (controlled emotions) and many refer to it as a soft skill. A leader that practices this skill is called the "touchy-feely type." Empathy definitely has a place in the medical profession, psychoanalysts, and counselors. The great thing about empathy is that it does not have to be complicated. It's about caring and taking notice of what is going on in a person's life. Simon Sinek, makes the case that empathy can be expressed in simple words, "Is everything Ok?" Empathy is an essential tool in a leaders' toolbox that should never be neglected.

"Be alert and of sober mind. Your enemy the devil prowls around like a roaring lion looking for someone to devour."

— I Peter 5:8 (NIV)

V= Vigilant: The definition of vigilant is the action or state of keeping a careful watch for possible danger or difficulties. This core value is not frequently demonstrated in leadership circles today. Nonetheless, vigilance is one of the significant traits that leaders need to have themselves or the core member(s) of their team should exhibit this behavior.

Vigilant leaders and team members pay close attention to not only what is happening on center stage, but what is happening on the fringes of the organization. Their inquisitiveness and watchfulness help to evade dangers with impending changes on the horizon. It is through their foresight and visionary approach that these leaders have the capacity and ability to see and act to prevent problems that could negatively impact the organizational goals.

According to Jim Collins, author of *Good to Great*, "Vigilant leaders produce a culture of people receptive to unearthing innovation of new ideas and opportunities. While exploring intensely, they can be content with vagueness, when conflicting ideas become a part of the dialogue."[31] In other words, they are not in a rush to reach a conclusion.

"The buck stops here."

— Harry S. Truman

A= Accountable: This famous quote by President Truman speaks to the essence of what it means to be accountable. Truman's words were his way of letting others know of his decision to take full responsibility for his administration's actions or inaction. Truman held himself to a higher standard if for no other reason, to be an example to those under his leadership. If a leader is not willing to wear the cloak of accountability, no matter how gifted or intelligent he is, failure and strife may be looming in the distance. Every leader should have accountability goals and objectives for themselves, as part of their PLDGP so that when things do not go according to plan, he cannot blame others.

As was noted, no one is perfect and every leader will make mistakes from time to time. Therefore, authentic leaders must accept the consequences of their decisions and empower someone inside or outside of their organization to hold them accountable as well. Someone who can freely speak the truth to the person in power. Speaking truth to power does not diminish or belittle the leader's value. On the flip side of the coin, leaders get better when they are willing to set aside their vanity and acknowledge what role they played in a failing situation. Accountable leaders are those who step up to the plate and take responsibility for their actions. Effective leadership necessitates authentic accountability.

"Intellectual growth should commence at birth and cease only at death."

— Albert Einstein

L= Life-Long Learner: Since we live in a world that is constantly changing, leaders must continue to expose themselves to knowledge. Whether it is in a formal or informal setting, personal and professional development should be a priority to remain relevant. The reality is that we forget 90% of what we learn over time. Therefore, the need to replenish becomes necessary to function at a high level. Researchers have found that 50% of people never read a book after they graduate from high school. That's insane! Granted, you will never know everything there is to know even if you are an expert in your field but you must invest in a life-long learning process. According to various articles and interviews, some of the most successful leaders in the world read often; Warren Buffet reads 500 pages per day, Bill Gates reads 50 books a year and Mark Cuban reads three hours a day.[32] Authentic leaders are life-long learners.

"Understanding is much deeper than knowledge. There are many people who know us, but very few who understand us."

— Unknown

U= Understanding: When it comes to building relationships understanding can be paramount in whether there will be success or failure. Elenora Roosevelt said, "Understanding is a two-way street." Most leaders want their teams to understand their point(s) of view and get on board with their vision and plans. The challenge comes when leaders are unwilling to go the extra mile to see and hear beyond what they think they already know. Understanding others can open a whole new world of thoughts and ideas that may have never been up for consideration. When we are trying to understand others, the first thought should be, they are human beings with value.

Of course, it is almost impossible to understand someone if you don't have a relationship with them at some level. If we don't give weight to understanding others, we can easily develop a dislike for those that we don't understand, and common ground becomes even harder. Understanding yourself and others is a necessary character trait for your toolbox.

"Right is right even if everyone is against it,

and wrong is wrong even if everyone is for it."

— William Penn

E= Ethical: The bottom line for ethical leaders is that they do the right thing for the right reason. Ethical leaders have within their core to be fearless to do what is right even if they are shunned by the majority. They can't stick their heads in the sand and pretend things are right for the sake of convenience. People who follow ethical leaders never have to be concerned about being disrespected, treated unfairly and unjust by their leader. Even though ethical leaders may not treat all followers the same, they treat everyone fairly. They operate from a place of honesty and transparency and focus on win-win outcomes for their organization. Under ethical leadership, the group not only endures but flourishes to a successful level.

"He is no fool who gives what he cannot keep,

to gain what he cannot lose."

— Jim Elliott

S= Steward: Many have come to know of the words steward or stewardship from a theological belief, where we are entrusted to take care of the world and manage all of the resources that God has provided. The understanding is that God expects believers to oversee all that God brings into their lives in a way that it reverends Him. Christians have come to recognize that they are only the steward and God is the owner. A foundational Scripture is found in Psalm 24:1 "The earth is the Lord's and all its fullness, the world and those who dwell therein."

There is a strong link for leaders being good stewards in their role as they intentionally take the responsibility of looking out for the wellbeing of their team. This well-being is exhibited when the leader purposely ensures that their team members are finding contentment in what they bring to the table. As a steward, the leader's responsibility is to get the right people on the bus and in the right seats. As difficult as it may be, an effort has to be made in this area to ensure the team remains motivated and the group is unified. Stewardship is a core value that will likely come under the heading in a leader's job description; "other duties as assigned." Authentic leaders are good stewards over their organization's assets and team.

As you are striving in your authentic journey, keep these Core Values on hand to ensure that you remain committed to becoming a better leader. Remember, it's through your actions, not thoughts that you become authentic in leadership and all of your relationships.

Chapter 6: Core Values - Personal Leadership Development

Authentic Checkup

1. Which of the Core Values rings true to your heart? Explain.

2. Describe an incident where you failed to be open-minded and the organization had a setback. What can you do differently going forward?

3. Team members have a strong desire to follow empathetic leaders. What steps have you implemented or plan to implement to demonstrate your commitment to empathetic leadership?

4. Who is your accountability partner and why? Name an instance where this person held you accountable. If you do not have an accountability partner, why not?

5. Vigilance is needed in leadership. Describe how you have been vigilant in advancing your organization and utilizing other Core Values to succeed.

PART IV:
Building Relationships

CHAPTER 7

RELATIONSHIPS MATTER

"If you want to go quickly, go alone and if you want to go far, go with others."
—African Proverb

Relationships and Leadership

From the opening chapter of the Bible in the book of Genesis the theme is clear, "Two are better than one." God made it clear when He spoke to Adam and said, "it is not good that man should be alone: I will make you a helper comparable to him."[33] No man or woman is an island unto himself. We were created for one partnership, collaboration, and relationship. Adam had Eve and the Lone Ranger had Tonto. This is true in every aspect of life. Rarely are individuals successful when they operate in a solo position. We were not meant to isolate ourselves. Isolation divides, hinders growth, creates stress and stagnates human beings of every creed and color. Taking the posture of going solo is against the principle that God spoke to Adam in the Garden of Eden.

Leaders who operate in isolation often accomplish very little by themselves. Since leaders must be many things to many people, it is important to recognize that every relationship is different because every person is different. In fact, people are often different on any given day with all their quirks so you have to be mindful of which person will show up on any given day. However, to be authentic means leaders have core beliefs and values that should remain intact despite who they interact with or what they are going through. Those beliefs should be hinged on the common ground of humanity, for every person the leader encounters despite that person's status on the totem pole.

Peter Drucker writes, "There's one characteristic common to all leaders—followers."[34] Remember, the definition of a leader is someone who has followers. David Gergen stated, "At the heart of leadership is the leader's relationship with followers. People will entrust their hopes and dreams to another person only if they think the other is a reliable vessel."[35]

When it comes to relationships and leadership you cannot have one without the other. Or can you? In our world today, there is a significant emphasis on the need for credible and competent leadership whereby individuals can reach common goals. Leadership is the be-all and end-all as it relates to how effective and productive groups of people can work together as they seek to make a difference in their endeavors collectively.

In 2019 "Doing Life Together" was our church theme. In an opening letter to the staff at the 2019 Retreat, our Pastor and First Lady said, "The heart of God is for each of us to have healthy relationships with one another like the early church did in the book of Acts 2:42, "And they continued steadfastly in the apostles' doctrine and fellowship in the breaking of bread and in prayers.[36] While doing research for this book I developed a working definition of "Authentic Relationships" based on the Scriptures.

Authentic relationships are existing relationships birthed out of collaborative trust, integrity, honesty, and accountability as individuals transparently interact with each other in their daily connections. When it comes to authentic relationships, leaders can often spot inauthentic behavior in others, but rarely see it in themselves. For far too many leaders there is a propensity to perpetrate a fraud and pretend to be more than they really are as they interact with each other. Inauthentic behavior is telling people what they want to hear or conforming to the expectations of others to gain acceptance or favor. This, in turn, leads to deception, duplicity, and dysfunction in the relationship. In the long run, credibility is lost and mistrust is adopted. Ultimately, this leads to a disconnection that will destroy the relationship and have a negative impact on overall workplace culture.

Herein lies the rub. Relationship-building is difficult work at best on any level. Building Authentic Relationships is especially difficult because there is always that human element that challenges leaders to be true to who they are, to "walk the talk" in every aspect of life. People will watch the leader walk before listening to their talk. Authentic relationships operate on a two-way street because these relationships are built on mutual respect and reciprocity. With these attributes as a driving force, there is a change in the game that leads to a deal or no deal. Quite simply, all bets are off.

Building Healthy Relationships

Which is more important, relationships or leadership or which should come first relationship or leadership? It's like that old adage "which came first the chicken or the egg?" The realization is that without the chicken there is no egg and without the egg, there is no chicken. The bottom line is that leaders should not negate one over the other if the goal is to be effective and have a positive impact. So, the question becomes can there be a healthy culture of leadership without healthy relationships? Or should I say can leaders lead effectively and not be relational? The answer to the question is empathically, no!

Study after study has revealed a critical component of competency for a leader is the ability to build and maintain healthy relationships. Yet one of the most under-emphasized and misunderstood factors in leadership is how can leaders accomplish this task. Relationships need to be cultivated and maintained at all costs because relationships are critical to the leader's success and to the success of those they lead. When the relationships are stable, the people working together are more interconnected. One of the biggest mistakes a leader can make is to think that the head is more important than the heart. When leaders lead from the heart, they are better able to form relationships. These leaders understand the African Proverb; "If you want to quickly, go alone and if you want to go far go with others."

Some leaders say this relationship-building is "soft" and they don't really have time to commit to this type of "soft stuff." Sooner or later the leader will be blindsided when morale becomes low, there is a high turnover, and disengagement among those in the ranks. As the follower's commitment is in a downward spiral, it is at this point the leader must ask if I do not have time for relationships do, I really have time to lead? When the leader gives up the relationship role then the leadership is short-lived, although the leader may still have the title or position.

John Maxwell points out this truth when he said, "There is no substitute for a relational foundation with your team. In all my life, I have never met a great leader who did not possess good relational skills. They are the most important abilities in leadership."[37] Therefore, the need to build and cultivate relationships is vital not only for success but also for survival. Dr. Joseph Umidi, Professor at Regent University, argues the point that relationships are of fundamental importance to bring about change in leaders,

> "I've been querying leaders for a number of years about what actually has transformed their lives, and the results are remarkably consistent. When I asked a group to jot down "two things" that changed your life, after which you were never the same. Participants almost never report an instance involving a seminar, conference, class or informational training event. Conversely, almost every individual selects one of the following two types of experiences as most transformational: 1) overcoming a difficult set of circumstances or 2) a significant relationship. Christian leaders virtually always point to experiences and relationships as most transforming, and rarely to the kind of formal training events that we customarily set up to produce change."[38]

As leaders climb the ladder of success in their organizations, one of the lessons they soon learn is that their educational training becomes less important and their relational skills take priority. Now, I want to be clear I am not saying that education does not play a significant role leadership success, as it unquestionably does, however, whether you are working with a sizable group or small group of people at the end of the day your relational skills will make all the difference in your rise or fall.

Leaders who build authentic relationships intentionally prioritize their energy on putting people first and product second—treating people like human beings, not like a pawn on a chessboard. You've probably heard the saying, "People don't quit their jobs, they quit their bosses." The mindset of an authentic leader is that every encounter is an opportunity to enhance their relationship with the person they encounter.

In building authentic relationships, the leader is asking questions and listening attentively with fewer distractions as possible. The leader is engaging the person to the point the person knows they have the leader's full attention.

In William George's book, A*uthentic Leadership,* he shares,

> "The detached style of leadership will not be successful in the twenty-first century. Today's employees demand more personal relationships with their leaders before they will give themselves fully to their jobs. They insist on having access to their leaders, knowing that in the openness and depth of the relationship with their leaders, trust and commitment are built. If the leader does not take the opportunity to have access to the follower, it can be difficult and almost impossible to produce an authentic relationship."[39]

It has been my observation that when a leader does not mesh with their team because of the disconnect in their relationships, this will have a significant impact on the growth and development of the overall team and the vision being carried out. There are no winners because the leader's nor the team's expectations are not being met. Therefore, productivity and transformation suffer in the long run.

The Relational VAT Principles

For those of you familiar with the Value Added Tax or VAT Tax, which is a tax on consumer goods and services, I want to change the acronym to mean, V= Vulnerable, A=Accountable, and T=Transparent to show how these three factors can bring about transformation and real value to a leaders' relationships in the church and the workplace. The three factors are essential to effective leadership. Despite the myths associated with these factors, workplaces have been known to thrive and flourish when the leaders embrace and promote them as qualities that make for successful relationships.

In a sense, vulnerability, accountability, and transparency all require a level of submission and surrendering to someone in the leader's sphere of influence. Let me build my case starting with the word: Vulnerable. In many circles, the word vulnerable is linked to people who are seen as wimps, weak and have lost control. By allowing themselves to be perceived as not acting as a strong leader when they publicly admit they have made mistakes and are taking responsibility for their shortcomings.

Vulnerability

Well, the truth of the matter is everyone has a weakness or two. We are damaged goods, cracked and bruised. If there were a choice in the matter, every person would seek do-overs without fear of repercussions at some point in their career. In the workplace and beyond there is a need to acknowledge and embrace that everyone falls short at one stage or another. This is what gives us license to be a part of humanity with warts and still build trusting relationships with one another.

In the book, *Getting Naked*, Patrick Lencioni buttresses my point by saying "Vulnerability, is one of the most undervalued and misunderstood of all human qualities. Without the willingness to be vulnerable, we will not build deep and lasting relationships in life. That's because there is no better way to earn a person's trust than by putting ourselves in a position of unprotected weakness and demonstrating that we believe they will support us."[40]

The truth is in adding value, all relationships need some level of vulnerability to be truly authentic. In my research, I found many credible definitions of what it means to be vulnerable. According to University of Houston Professor Brene' Brown leading researcher on vulnerability, says "it is the birthplace of love, belonging, joy, courage, empathy, ad creatively. It is the source of hope, empathy, accountability, and authenticity."[41]

Exploring all of the definitions I came across my summation for being vulnerable and its significance to be a healthy leader is the ability to open up to the possibility of being judged, rejected, and hurt, by unmasking and revealing one's true self with all of their weaknesses. The challenge comes in how individuals handle their weaknesses that show up in life from time to time. In moments of crisis, leaders should let those they lead know that they may not have the answers, but as a team, they can figure it out together.

A great story of vulnerability is seen in Bill George's, *True North: Discover Your Authentic Leadership*. George shares the story of Tad Piper former Chairman and CEO of Piper Jaffray as he went through a tough and strenuous time in his firm. In the end, the only way he was able to overcome the problem he was facing was a willingness to be vulnerable with his team and admit the mistakes that had been made and take responsibility for them. Piper shared, "My wife and I decided to be completely honest with them and totally vulnerable. We showed that we were real people, feeling just like they were. We stood in front of them and told them we were scared. I also talked about my chemical dependency and about my faith. That was the most powerful thing we have ever done. People never forgot that day because we showed our vulnerability. All of sudden everybody on our team trusted us, even the skeptics."[42]

The lesson for all leaders to learn is being vulnerable can be the catalyst for building trusting relationships. When leaders are honest and make it clear that they do not walk around with an "S" on their chest members of their team know they are human, just like they are and are prone to failure on any given day. When a leader is willing to be vulnerable, they are making a shift and moving out of their safety zone. Yes, it means taking a risk, going out on a limb, opening up to reveal their true selves but at the end of the day, it is worth more than they could ever imagine.

Peter Scazzero's, *The Emotionally Healthy Church*, applies Biblical principles for Christian leaders to deal with life's relational challenges. "I learned that leadership is not always being the strong one; instead, it is being the weak one who is made strong by God alone."[43] Parenthetically, considerably too many men do not see vulnerability as being masculine. Consequently, they blanket women as being too emotional, after all, women are "the weaker sex," as often quoted from the Bible out of context. Therefore, vulnerability is not a trait that some male leaders aspire to achieve but they should.

More importantly, Scott Boren's, *The Relational Way,* advises that "we must follow the authority demonstrated by Christ. He displayed vulnerable power. When God pulled back the veil between man and himself, he came as a servant of servants, the weakest of all."[44] Through Christ's display of weakness and vulnerability He was able to connect with those He came to serve.

Accountability

The second factor that adds value to leaders' relationships is Accountability. I will briefly discuss accountability as we covered it in Chapter six as one of the core values in your personal leadership development process. Additionally, under the relationship banner, I want to expand the topic to include a few more thoughts. In essence, accountability is taking responsibility for what one agrees to do. First, healthy leaders should give at least one person in their personal and professional life, permission to hold them accountable. If those who lead don't have someone to be accountable to, it really means the leader has no one in their lives that can speak truth to them, and the leader is not speaking truth to anyone. Secondly, the leader should be holding members of their team accountable. Every leader and follower stand on dangerous ground if they are not being held accountable and if they are not holding others accountable. I call it the "Held and Hold Principle" which leaders need both to have successful outcomes. When leaders do not hold their team members accountable there could be signs of managerial dysfunction especially if favoritism or nepotism is involved. On the other hand, leaders must use sound reasoning and not hold team members accountable for matters beyond their control. Once again, as it relates to a healthy leader, they do not shun being held accountable, especially when they are clear they are walking in their purpose.

Actually, such leaders embrace accountability with the understanding that their example can have a transforming effect on others and the organization. It is one thing for a leader to assume responsibility for their actions, yet it is on the next level for a leader to welcome accountability and not see it as a weight around their necks but as a duty and an obligation. Particularly when the leader has made some mistakes and there is a call for a clean-up on aisle nine.

When leaders are willing to apologize and make amends for their behavior, they can change the trajectory of the organization. These leaders can inspire and motivate others to walk in their shoes. When there are honest levels of accountability, it signals there are true and sincere relationships in place. Every team needs honesty to be prevalent in the culture. Is that not we learned at our parent's knee? Leaders and followers must comprehend that caring also means confronting people with the reality of their situations. It means dealing with issues head-on, not beating around the bush. Paul tells us, "If someone in your group does something wrong, you who are spiritual should go to that person and gently make him right again."[45] Leaders cannot take the posture that they don't want to rock-the-boat or ruffle anyone's feathers. As you have come to realize, leadership is more than a title and it can frequently carry uncomfortable responsibilities.

Transparency

The final bookend and third factor that adds value to relationships in the church and the workforce is Transparency. The sign of true transparency is open and honest communication. While transparency can be problematic and unpleasant for some, often the benefits to the whole team overshadow difficult times. Transparency is developing a culture where everyone in the organization is respected. Followers respect the leaders and the leaders respect the followers. Everyone has a voice, and everyone is encouraged to use their voice in respectful ways.

Transparency for successful leaders is not something that is done occasionally, nor it is seen as one-sided. Creating a transparent environment is a win-win for everyone on the team in their daily interactions. Not only should transparent communication be encouraged, but there should also be clear expectations that everyone will contribute value without being opaque, sugar-coating or have ulterior motives. Members of the team can be more effective and work together more efficiently when the value is given to what everyone brings to the table.

Millennials, Gen Xers and Gen Z's that are rapidly populating the workforce, have high expectations of transparency. Where there is an environment of expectations, people usually step up to the plate, knowing that their input could have an impact on the organization reaching its goals. Complete "sunshine" as my grandmother used to say. Jeff Weiner, CEO of LinkedIn believes it is best to be open about company matters good or bad. Letting the employees know they have nothing to hide. He does this through building on transparency by holding bi-weekly meetings where he updates the employees on company matters and listens to their suggestions. Weiner asks open-ended questions that require more than a yes or no answer i.e., "what do you think?" No questions about the company should be off-limits unless they are related to an individual personal matter.

The truth is transparency builds trust and the lack of transparency can destroy trust. If transparency is not promoted by the senior leaders first, everyone in the organization is left to draw their own conclusions on the matters at hand, and the situations can often be translated worse than what is really going on. Get rid of the so-called company lingo and speak from the heart. In order to get transparency from the team, the leader must demonstrate it to the team and encourage them for their input. The most disconcerting and disappointing thing a leader can do is to open the door to feedback from their team and not respect it, ignore it, or not find a way to respond to the feedback. The value added here is that it shows the team not only are their skills valuable but their ability to think and have input is welcome and appreciated.

Keep in mind that too much transparency can be just as damaging as not enough. As with everything in life, there needs to be balance. Every situation is not meant for public consumption. Leaders and followers are not expected to air all their dirty laundry at the staff meetings, or with everyone they interact on the job. Mature people understand the need to be transparent, with full disclosure in some matters, however, this should be done with those you trust, and you know that they have your best interest at heart.

In closing, I offer two cautionary tales of being transparent. First, be clear that being transparent is revealing your weaknesses, your mistakes, and your faux pas'. Not someone else's under any circumstances! This speaks to the height of betrayal and is unethical. Second, beware there are those who will seek to take advantage of your weaknesses and flaws only for their personal gain. Everyone cannot be a part of the inner circle where there is full disclosure. The Bible teaches us that familiarity breeds contempt. Yes, confession is good for the soul, but not with every soul. Everyone is not mature enough nor does everyone have the wisdom to keep confidences. When it comes to being transparent organizations need to be able to protect everyone's private information such as compensation, or personal matters, and only share certain information on a need to know basis while ensuring confidentiality. When all is said and done, transparency will yield a way of "Doing Life Together" that produces ethical churches and workplaces. Leadership is a tough job, therefore, it requires tough skin in any and all situations.

Relationship Wealth

What is "Relationship Wealth?" When we hear the word "wealth" we often relate it to how much money, property or material things a person may have. But the reality is that wealth comes in many forms and "relationship wealth" is worth more than silver and gold. I first heard this expression from my godmother, Reverend Willie Taplin Barrow, who was a woman of great wisdom. She died at the age of 92. She never met a stranger and treated everyone the same. She was the personification of relationship wealth.

Reverend Barrow was a woman of great faith. She was the type of woman that you didn't just meet, you experienced her presence. Without any pretense she made everyone feel special because she was genuinely interested in people of every race or hue. I have never met a woman who valued relationships more than her. People loved to be around her because she was the real deal— authentic from sunup to sundown. I watched her interactions across this country literally with President's, high government officials foreign and domestic, hotel maids, and waiters in restaurants and her demeanor was always the same. More often than not when we ate at a restaurant and she asked for the bill, it had already been paid.

Far too many leaders fail to realize the wealth we have in our relationships until it is too late. There are people in our lives that bring a wealth of love, knowledge, and wisdom but we take it for granted that they will always be there. When they are gone we realize that we should have spent more time gleaning from them. One of the lessons leaders need to learn before it's too late is building our relationships with family, friends, and co-workers, is that everyone has value, and everyone needs to be respected at the moment they are in our presence and beyond. This is the key to true joy and happiness for those who strive to be authentic in their relationships. To make a difference in someone's life you don't have to be wise, rich, or beautiful (by the world's standards), you just have to show up as your *real* self. Yes, relationships do matter in whatever form they come in.

Chapter 7 - Relationships Matter

Authentic Relationships

1. What steps do you take to build relationships with people in your church or in your workplace? Name at least two.

2. On a scale of 1-10, (10 being the highest), how important is it to you to be in authentic relationships?

3. Provide your definition of a healthy and unhealthy relationship.

4. After reading this chapter on Relationships Matter, what skills/ behavior do you need to add or remove?

____

____

____

____

5. When it comes to the VAT Factors, share in one sentence (for each) how you have experienced being: Vulnerable, Accountable, and Transparent?

____

____

____

____

6. Can you name one person you admire who is wealthy in relationships and why?

____

____

____

____

PART V

Character & Leadership Foundation

"How come when dad has to weed
it's 'a waste of his time', but when
I have to weed it's 'building my character'?"

CHAPTER 8

PART I: CAST OF CHARACTERS LEADERSHIP FOUNDATION

"Be careful of your thoughts, for your thoughts become your words; Be careful of your words, for your words become your deeds; Be careful of your deeds for your deeds become your habits; Be careful of your habits, for your habits becomes your character; Be careful of your character, for your character becomes your destiny."[46]

- ***Anonymous***

In 1985 Tina Turner won a Grammy for the Song of the Year, "What's Love Got to do With It?" In her lyrics, she describes love as a second-hand emotion. She downplayed the importance of love. This is not the case with love nor is it the case for character when it comes to authentic leaders' relationships. One extremely important aspect of authentic relationships is that the leader soon learns that their reputation is what they are perceived to be, and their character is who they are without filters.

In many cases when churches and workplaces are looking for leaders their first thought is often to seek leaders that have high Intelligence Quotient (IQ). They look for those whose skill sets include, being a good communicator, able to cast vision, creativity, and marketing abilities, just to name a few. Yet the reality is that none of those skill sets will make a productive and healthy leader if they don't have good character. More than ever before good character is regarded as a critical element for leaders to maintain credibility.

Character versus Competency

"Leadership is a potent combination of strategy and character. But if you must be without one—be without strategy." [47]

— Norman Schwarzkopf

As with any topical research on the word "character," it will yield several definitions as well as millions of books, magazines, and quotes on the subject matter. I chose to use the following definition from Reference.com: "Character consists of a person's mental or moral disposition manifested by his interaction with his environment and with others."[48] Think of it as the totality of a person's well-defined behaviors positive and negative. Examples of positive character includes optimism, happiness and ambitious. Negative character includes dishonesty, cruelty, and selfishness. Developing a healthy posture of character can be difficult as it takes a daily conscious effort, to say nothing of maintaining it.

Merriam-Webter.com defines character as "the way someone thinks, feels and behaves." I want to drive this thought further and talk about Character versus Competency, in which there has been much debate. As I stated earlier, too often in our work culture the focus is on hiring the brightest and the best as it relates to skills or competency. Conversely, what tends to happen is that some leaders overlook flaws. Leaders need to be mindful, to hold those who display bad character accountable, and not let them get away with their negative behavior because of their talent and authority in the establishment. In the long run, this will diminish the credibility of the leader and the credibility of the organization will suffer.

Unfortunately, too many leaders assume that the character flaws in a competent worker will never outweigh the need for a person that is extremely effective at doing their job. The truth is competency can bring high acclaim at the job but it does not necessarily make a healthy leader. The bottom line is that leaders need to look for a balance in character and competency in those they bring on the team especially if they will serve in a leadership capacity. The negative impact of an absence of character, or a flawed character, will continuously be larger than the competency or skill set a person brings to the table. For healthy working environments to exist, those making the decision who to hire must, be more focused on character than competency.

The reality is that you can teach a person competency skills, but it is much harder to develop character in people if they have no sense of morals or ethics. When leaders do not take time to help a person develop character, the monetary cost and human carnage (emotional damage) they leave in their wake can often never be recouped. Regrettably, there emerges a contradiction in many organizations as to what we espouse as significant to operations versus what we tolerate.

Character Traits

A person's character is what makes them who they are. The Bible teaches us in Proverbs 23:7 "For as he thinks in his heart; so is he." A person of great character takes a stand for what is right and does not abdicate his position despite the consequences he may face. A leader's character is established in the choices they make. It has been said that you can judge a person's character based upon how they treat people who have nothing to offer them in return.

Character is the groundwork of leadership and will ultimately determine the success of every leader. In Dr. Martin Luther King Jr.'s, "I Have a Dream" speech, he stated, "I have a dream that my four little children will one day live in a nation where they will not be judged by the color of their skin, but by the content of their character." Here Dr. King pointed out the fact that character, an internal quality, is more important than a person's outward appearance.

Dr. Howard Hendricks, a long-time professor at Dallas Theological Seminary, shares his observation with Aubrey Malphurs in an interview in the book, *Being Leader,* "The greatest crisis in the world today is a crisis of leadership and the greatest crisis of leadership is a crisis of character." Good character is built on a leader's sound moral compass that is based on Core Values discussed previously. Leaders that are in touch with who they are, and what they represent, will always receive respect from their team and others based not on personality but a sincere heart. A leader's character can sway followers in a way that they are motivated or disillusioned as it relates to how they perform in the organization.

In I Peter 1:5-8, we see character as a building block process into our lives:

> "For this reason, make every effort to add to your faith goodness, and to goodness, knowledge, and to knowledge, self-control; and to self-control, perseverance; and to perseverance, godliness, and to godliness, mutual affection, love. For if you possess these qualities in increasing measure, they will keep you from being ineffective and unproductive in your knowledge of our Lord Jesus Christ."

Therefore, this Scripture can be seen as the remedy for immorality and exploitation for those lacking character in our workplaces and churches. While many leaders are determined to be successful, not all leaders are willing to do the difficult work to build their character. William George makes the case when he says, "many leaders who are driven to achieve often skip or short cut the hard work of character development and the cultivation of self-awareness that is characterized by authentic leaders. By not doing the hard work, these leaders can be very destructive."[49]

There are important character traits that symbolize authentic leadership. These traits should be evident for those who are current leaders, as well as those who are preparing for future leadership roles. As I plowed through my research, I was able to determine three-character traits that rose to the top of the list, as it relates to what character traits people look for and admire in their leaders. Those three traits are: trust, integrity and loyalty. Trust is the overarching bridge to Building Authentic Relationships.

Moreover, leaders who function with trust were also known to exhibit integrity and loyalty. In S. Michie and J. Gooty's central thesis is that authentic leaders behave in ways that reflect self-transcendent values such as honesty, loyalty and equality." [50] Therefore, I am positing, that if a person is not trustworthy, they will not have integrity and if they do not have integrity, they will not have genuine loyalty.

Character Foundation Trust

"Few things can help an individual more than to place responsibility on him, and to let him know that you trust him."

— Booker T. Washington

For the purpose of our discussion it is key to draw comparisons between the words, *"trust," "trustworthy," "truthfulness," "honesty," and "trustor,"* due to the close association these words have to each other. These words will be used interchangeably to prove the necessity of building trust in our relationships. One constant in every healthy relationship is the foundation of trust. If leaders want sustainable accomplishments and want those who follow them to fully commit to their assigned jobs, the trust factor is essential. Solid trusting relationships are built with an investment of time (there is often some trial and error to get it right), resources, and effort to discover common ground between the parties. Trust is that special ingredient that will ensure you are building a winning team.

When leaders are inclined to move forward beginning with positive expressions and deeds, the process of forming trusting relationships can be developed. As the trust factor is being built among leaders and followers there is an expectation that each group will act in harmony in their previous and present interactions at the center of the organization's goals and objectives. As the parties strengthen their relationships through continuous communication, and interfacing, more trust is extended to the point where there is less suspicion that either party will violate the common shared values that bring benefits to each other as well as their organizations.

Stephen M.R. Covey bolsters my argument when he says, "Relationships of all kinds are built on and sustained by trust. They can also be broken and destroyed by lack of trust. Try to imagine any meaningful relationship without trust. In fact, low trust is the very definition of a bad relationship."[51] Therefore, I believe the above propositions related to trust helps to explain how and why authentic leaders form trusting and cooperative relationships with their followers. To earn trust, a leader needs to be authentic in their interactions.

Trust in the workforce is critical to the overall achievements of the organization and the team. It is essential for leaders to comprehend that trust is part of every objective, every encounter, and with every member on the team because it has a major impact on outcomes. What many leaders don't fully grasp is that people who do not trust their leaders are not giving their best. Leaders may feel that their employee's production is high but the truth is that it could be much higher when follower(s) are giving their all, not just for compensation. When the rubber meets the road, the reality is that money is only a means to an end of one's victories, not the other way around.

Colin Powell's book, *It Worked For Me: In Life and Leadership*, makes a profound statement in the chapter, "Trust Your People." He writes, "They will follow you because they trust you. They will follow you because they believe in you and they believe in what they have to do. So, everything you do as a leader, must focus on building trust in a team. Trust among the leaders, trust among the followers, and trust between the leaders and the followers. And it begins with the selfless, trusting leaders." [52] Trust is often cited as a trademark of effective relationships. Without trust, leader's relationships will not achieve the highest level of effectiveness.

"The best way to find out if you can trust somebody is to trust them."

— *Ernest Hemmingway*

Trust is a two-way street. While leaders want to feel that their followers trust them, followers must also feel that they are trusted by their leaders. It all comes down to the fact that leaders and followers should carry themselves in a way that shows they can be trusted. Trust must be earned from both sides of the fence. Trust is a core value that sustains relationships. One of the greatest accolades a person on the team can give to the other is "I trust you."

A great definition of "trust" comes from R.C. Mayer when he writes that it "is willingness to be vulnerable to the actions of another party based on the expectation that the other will perform a particular action important to the trustor."[53] Mayer picks up on the theme of vulnerability which is discussed in a previous chapter as it is a major part of trust in relationships. In addition, Patrick Lencioni's *The Advantage: Why Organizational Health Trumps Everything Else in Business,* introduces the concept of vulnerability-based trust.

> "The kind of trust that is necessary to build a great team is what I call vulnerability-based trust. This is what happens when members get to a point where they are completely comfortable being transparent, honest, and naked with one another, where they say and genuinely mean things like "I screwed up," "I need help," "Your idea is better than mine," "I wish I could learn to do that as well as you do," and even, "I'm sorry." [54]

The necessity for trust arises from our interdependence with one another. What tends to happen is there is a reciprocal effect in the relationship of the person who is being trusted, that they feel the need to act accordingly in trusting others based on the trust that has been provided to him. Trust becomes indispensable in our social interactions and is a reciprocal component in relationships. Truthfulness is critical for daily life within the church and the workplace. If trust is abandoned, then the answer is known, but until then, as leaders we should give others the benefit of our trust.

Trust and Competence

Trust and competence go hand-in-hand as attributes that people look for and respect in their leaders. The more we perceive competence in an individual, the more likely we are to develop some level of trust in them. Kouzes and Posner make the point by stating, "If you don't believe in the Messenger, you won't believe the Message." [55] Leaders build trust by representing factual information in who they are and what they say and do. Competence brings personal confidence and public credibility to the leader.

Organizational guru Stephen M. R. Covey followed in his father's footsteps picking up on the theme of competence in *The Speed of Trust: The One Thing That Changes Everything.* "Trust is a function of two things: Character and Competence. Character includes your integrity, your motives, and your intent with people. Competence includes your capabilities, your skills, your results, and your track record. And both are vital."

M. R. Covey goes on to say,

> "While it may not come naturally for us to think of trust in terms of character, it is equally important that we also learn to think in terms of competence. Think about it; people trust people who make things happen. They give the new curriculum to their most competent instructors. They give the promising projects or sales leads to those who have delivered in the past. Recognizing the role of competence helps us identify and give language to underlying trust issues we otherwise can't put a finger on.[56]

In addition, Stephen R. Covey makes an argument for competence by stating,

> "Trustworthiness is more than integrity; it also connotes competence. In other words, you may be an honest doctor, but before I trust you, I want to know that you're competent as well.

> We sometimes focus too much on integrity and not enough on personal competence and professional performance. Honest people who are incompetent in their area and they profess being an expertise are not trustworthy.[57]

George Barna rounds out the thoughts on being competent in *Leaders on Leadership* in a chapter entitled, "Nothing is More Important Than Leadership." Barna describes one of the characteristics that he believes every Christian leader should have which is to possess functional competencies and abilities that must allow him to perform the tasks demanded of his position." [58]

Trust should not be viewed in a "Pollyannaish" perspective. I want to be clear that trusting relationships do not always end with a happy ever after report. When trust is broken it can produce enormous amounts of stress and anxiety that is not easy to overcome. Repairing damaged relationships from broken trust can be very difficult. However, from my years of counseling and coaching, I believe repair can come in two forms: reconciliation and/or forgiveness or both. It is my opinion that in order to repair broken trust there must first be a need to forgive as there may not always be a place to reconcile the relationship back to before the infraction.

Integrity

"At the end of the day, people with integrity
have one thing in common they sleep well."

— Don Graham

Integrity has garnered increasing media and public attention due to a decline in the moral standards of leaders in every corner of our society. In a study by Kouzes and Posner in *Credibility,* they revealed "the most desired characteristic in a leader was integrity." [59] Not much has changed since Kouzes and Posner, *Credibility,* in 2011. And the general public is less and less tolerant of leader's unethical behavior as it continues to rise. This speaks to the old axioms "the more things change, the more they remain the same."

Everyone is clamoring for integrity from politicians, corporate executives, religious leaders, entertainers, sports icons, employers and employees. Stephen Carter said, "Integrity is a lot like the weather: everyone talks about it, but no one knows what to do about it." [60] There seems to be a great deal of confusion about what it is and how it is fostered. Noting the term "integrity" from the Latin word "*integritas*," with the root word being "*integer*" means "untouched, intact, entire." Integrity is defined in the Encarta Web site as "the quality of possessing firm principles and steadfastly adhering to high moral standards; wholeness; the state of being complete or undivided, firm adherence to a code, especially moral or artistic values, the quality or state of being complete or undivided." [61] The word integrity can be summed up in several ways:

- An individual who remains steadfast in doing what is right because of moral virtues.
- Having the attributes of being sincere and credible in your behavior.
- Your conduct is unswerving as you carry out valid ethical leadership.
- You are distinct in having your own values-initiated in decency and order.

A preliminary step to gaining a better understanding of integrity would be to settle on a meaning of the word for this discussion with the understanding that integrity is more than just being honest. Going forward I posit to adopt Stephen Carter's definition by using his three-step approach: "1) discerning what is right and what is wrong, 2) acting on what you have discerned, even at a personal cost, and 3) saying openly that you are acting on your understanding of right from wrong." [62] Although we can come up with many definitions and our own understanding of the word, when the rubber meets the road we can lean-in on the old adages "practice what you preach," which offers an elementary level understanding of what it means to be a person of integrity.

Integrity is often seen at its best not necessarily in normal times of life but mostly displayed in the crises of life in what is called "structural integrity." This is the same term that is used when speaking of a building that can remain standing during an earthquake, hurricanes, strong winds or other natural occurrences. The integrity of the building must be there before the storms hit, if not, it's too late to keep everything from collapsing.

People of integrity are proactive in a sense that they don't wait for a situation to occur, yet beforehand they have developed a deep resolve to live with integrity whatever situations may come their way. It is almost saying, I don't know every detail, or what I will do in every situation, but I do know exactly what I will not do, as it relates to conceding my principles. John Maxwell stated, "When I have integrity, my words and my deeds match up. I am who I am, no matter where I am or who I am with. He continued by saying, "People with integrity have nothing to hide and nothing to fear, their lives are an open book." [63]

Simply put, integrity is not what a person does, but more so who they are. In a real sense for persons with integrity, it is organic, it flows out of their personhood. Therefore, integrity becomes a by-product of character, which cannot be hidden because it "permeates" or seeps through an individual's life. Those leaders who are striving to be people of integrity clearly understand there is a dominant stream that cultivates honesty. Therefore, leaders of integrity work hard in fulfilling expectations without being duplicitous. In *2Corinthians 8:21*, The Apostle Paul makes a statement regarding collecting money in the church saying: "*Everything has been done honestly in the sight of God and man.*" (CWB) [64]

Followers also benefit from leaders with Integrity because they are straightforward in the sense that they may not treat everyone the same, but they treat everyone fairly and with respect and dignity. Leaders with integrity seek to create an environment where staff are never pressured to compromise their personal values in order to ensure bottom line profits are met. There are great benefits to followers when leaders' actions are based on principles-centered leadership. When leaders can act the same in every environment then those leaders are well on their way to living a life with authenticity and integrity.

Stephen Covey shares this perspective on integrity in his book *Principle-Centered Leadership* stating:

> "When we are true to the light we have been given, when we keep our word consistently, when we are striving continually to harmonize our habits with our value system, then our life is integrated. Our honor becomes greater than our moods, and we can have confidence in ourselves because we know ourselves. We know that we will be true and faithful under temptation. Integrity is the foundation of all true goodness and greatness." [65]

Now, this may appear to be an impossible task that Covey is espousing. The good news here is to be a person of integrity is not just for the so-called superstars of morality, those who seem to always get it right. No, it is for those who are striving, attempting, determined, and are intentional daily to be better for themselves and others. It's for those who know that there will be some missteps and try it again moments. In essence, these are the steps a leader takes in becoming authentic.

Another benefit of working alongside, a leader with integrity is when they find themselves in a situation where they are unclear of what to do next, particularity as they give guidance to their followers on assignments, they don't fall back on ambiguity. No, they fall forward communicating a *Core Value*, which in often consistency in their behavior. Consistent is a benchmark for leaders with integrity. In an article entitled; The True meaning of Integrity, So-young Kang shares her thoughts on consistency:

> "Consistency is about being the same regardless of the situation. For example, do you know of leaders whose mood changes by the day and make rash decisions on certain days, yet calm and engaging on other days? This would be an example of inconsistent actions and outcomes. Consistency is a choice that we make as leaders every single day, even when the situation or environment is not great. If you just had an argument with someone before walking into your next meeting, consistency means that you will make a conscious choice to shift gears and release yourself from the negativity of the last conversation and not bring that to the next meeting." [66]

When leaders make promises they are consistent to ensure they are kept and if unable to keep the promise they quickly make it known. This speaks to what Stephen Covey mentioned above. In fact, I believe leaders with integrity would rather under promise and over deliver.

Despite the fact that there may be some disagreements on the terminology, in the next chapter I will explore briefly some of the benefits followers gain from leaders with integrity and the harm those without integrity heap onto their followers. In my opening quote by Don Graham as it relates to those leaders who sleep well because they have an unobstructed conscience, may appear to be a small benefit, but it is actually priceless and can add years to your overall health and longevity.

Chapter 8 - Part F: Cast of Characters

Leadership Foundation

1. What character traits do you admire in the current leaders in your life? How has your leader's character affected you?

____

____

____

____

2. During your time in leadership has there been an incident where trust was broken? Were you able to restore it? Is so, how? If not, what lesson did you learn?

____

____

____

____

3. Would others consider you to be a person of integrity? If yes, give three reasons.

____

____

____

____

4. What type of plan do you envision will build trust among the team and active engagement?

____

____

____

____

5. General Colin Powell once said, "Loyalty means giving me your honest opinion whether you think I'll like it or not." Do you agree? Explain.

____

____

____

____

CHAPTER 9

PART II: CAST OF CHARACTERS ETHICAL AND UNETHICAL BEHAVIORS

"In looking for people to hire, you look for three qualities: integrity, intelligence, and energy. And, if they don't have the first, the other two will kill you."
— ***Warren Buffett***

Quiet as it may be kept, morality in any organization is dependent upon the ethical standards endorsed within the organization's culture. Whether it is ethical or unethical behavior, the light shines bright in either direction. Sooner or later a person will reveal what they stand for and followers have to govern themselves accordingly. Ethical leadership can bring out the best in people, and conversely unethical leadership can bring out the worst. To say nothing of the moral concerns that will inhabit the organization for the good and the bad. If the culture is viewed as supporting immoral behavior from the organization's leadership, then the ability to establish and maintain healthy relationships will not take root or quickly diminish.

It is critical to know which side of the fence you will stand on: ethical or unethical leadership. Both yield stark differences. Parker Palmer, stated, "A leader is a person who had an unusual degree of power to create the conditions under which other people must live and move and have their being, conditions that can be either be as illuminating as heaven or a shadowy as hell. A leader must take special responsibility for what's going on inside his or her own self, inside his or her consciousness, lest the act of leadership create more harm than good. [67] This thought prompts us to remember that leaders of integrity take full responsibility for their behavior whether there are positive or negative consequences. The notion also takes us back to the discussion on Personal Leadership Development and Knowing Oneself. This will always be a common thread as integrity connects to leadership behavior.

When leaders are not divided, they are not pretentious; what they reveal externally, is the same person internally. These leaders do not have to guard what they say for fear of being two-faced. Their story will always be the same despite who they are interacting with. They don't wait to see who is watching before they do what is right. In a Corporate Recruiters Research Survey from the University of Notre Dame, "1,509 employers in 51 countries were asked what primary traits and abilities they sought in MBA candidates. Again, integrity ranked in the top three of 18 identified attributes." [68]

For all of us, life is happening in real time; storms of life are buffering us, there are challenges in health, finances, family dilemmas, disappointments, distresses, and defeats come at you fast. Yet the great benefit of having leadership that operates with moral standards is that you can rest assured that their walk and talk are always the same. Even in hard times they maintain their integrity because they are not fraudulent in how they handle life's vicissitudes. The same way they handle the pressures of life when the sun is shining, is the same way they handle life when the storms are raging. Why? Because they are not double minded, and not willing to compromise their integrity even though things may be in disarray.

Organizations suffer when their leaders come up short not acting with integrity. The first and foremost consequence is that there is a lack of trust infused into the environment. T. Cunningham cited in his book, *Leadership 101: Integrity,* "A lack of trust is listed as the number one problem facing leaders today." [69] When trust is broken, it can be repaired, however, it is not easily regained. In instances where there is an unethical breach in the organization such as false claims, theft, or harassment, those in charge must address this behavior directly and without hesitation despite the level of the person involved. This will ensure there is no suspicion that anything is being covered up. Organizations must maintain their integrity by dealing with the issue of moral failure with a sense of urgency. We've heard it said before, "the cover-up is often worse than the crime."

Several years ago, I was told about a gentleman who has a terrible reputation among his family and peers. His behavior caused many disturbances in his family and on his job. This person was rude and disrespectful. He would openly criticize, berate and belittle those who were not on his level of seniority. What became interesting to me was the fact that people who knew about his repeated unethical behavior, particularly on his job, talked about the company he worked for and could not understand how he remained on his job. It seemed clear that everybody in the organization knew about this unethical behavior. Yet there was talk that he was an exceptional worker, so he was never reprimanded or terminated. However, because of his behavior, I was told that morale suffered from his actions and caused several productive people to leave the organization for a competitor.

Despite his "exceptional work," in order to silent the conversations at the water cooler and in the parking lot, this employee should have been dismissed or asked to resign. The organization should have made it clear to everyone that this unethical behavior will not be tolerated, and there are consequences that could lead to termination. Any leader or follower operating under the belief that the Code of Conduct or Code of Ethics of the organization does not apply to them should be in for a rude awakening. The bottom line is that if leaders are not vigilant on these kinds of sensitive matters, one or two bad apples operating without integrity can wreak havoc on the organization.

This was definitely seen in March 2019 when all major news outlets blasted the story about several Ivy League and top colleges in the nation accepting thousands of dollars from rich and famous parents to admit their kids into their desired school. The illegal and unethical scheme was carried out by a few perpetrators of an "Education Consulting Firm" and the athletic coaches of these top schools. Contractors of the consulting firm took the SAT's for students, arranged to be seated near students to provide answers to the SAT, and also paid school administrators, at the direction of the coaches, to change SAT scores. The consulting firm also Photoshopped photos and records of students engaged in athletic competition.

This continues to be a tremendous scandal and to date over 50 people have been arrested. Not only that, there were numerous articles online citing that "86 % of college students say they've cheated on a test, and many said, "It's easier than ever with mobile devices." [70] The integrity piece runs deep not only with parents cheating but students cheating as if this should be the norm. Why not? Everybody does it, is commonly spoken about in academic environments. This is disheartening. But the problem does not stop there. Duke University in North Carolina recently settled a faked-research lawsuit. "The private university submitted claims for dozens of research grants that contained falsified and fabricated information that unjustly drained taxpayer money from several government agencies. The school said it is repaying grant money and related penalties, which has amounted to 112 million dollars. The local U.S. Attorney Matthew G. T. Martin said in a statement; "We expect Duke researchers to adhere always to the highest standards of integrity and virtually all of them to do that with great dedication." [71]

Once unethical behavior has been uncovered there must be swift and clear communication detailing how the organization will enact policies to prevent similar incidents in the future. Many organizations struggle with communication which can cause unnecessary disruption and demotivation in the ranks. I have often heard it said particularly in times of uncertainty that leaders need to consistently communicate again and again to ensure that everyone is on the same page and receives the same message. No detail is too small when trying to increase confidence and goodwill among the team.

However, it takes more than communication for an organization to operate at the highest-level of integrity, where they not only strive, but flourish. Organizations must ensure that there are ethical standards communicated and demonstrated from the top down because once the leader sets the bar, those in the organization must follow it. If not, they will surely reap the consequences. The rise of credibility in an organization can take years to build up, however, the loss of credibility can be quickly tarnished with one or two bad tweets, Facebook comments, or Instagram photos.

It was reported that Tesla CEO Elon Musk lost his temper on a phone call to his stockholders. He made statements to people like, "boring and bonehead questions are not cool. Next?" Many people said Musk had an emotional breakdown. News of the call went viral on social media. Musk's fitness to run the company he founded was in question. Later, footage surfaced of Musk smoking marijuana on a podcast.

It caused quite a stir. Then, to add to Musk's leadership woes, in 2018 he sent out a series of Tweets that the SEC claimed misled investors and caused Tesla's stock to skyrocket. Musk and Tesla were fined 20 million each and Musk had to step down as Tesla's Chairman for three years.

Notwithstanding, some negative behavior by leaders can be productive, like anger. According to the article, "Go ahead. Get angry about Unethical Behavior." [72] The author is making the case that when leaders show anger, their followers want to see this behavior; "but only in reaction to addressing immoral behavior." In other words, followers want to see their leaders being authentic when they are willing to address unethical matters in the public arena, versus flying off the handle or having meltdowns, about personal idiosyncrasies, in the common day-to-day operations. All leaders have their quirks, but it is the leader's responsibility to manage them to the point that they don't allow their anger to spill over to abusive behavior. Proverbs 12:16 (NCV) says, "Fools quickly show that they are upset, but the wise ignore insults."

Christians can find some justification under the banner of what the Bible speaks to as Righteous Anger or Righteous Indignation. Paul refers to "putting off unrighteous anger" in the Scriptures. Leaders have a right to get angry over injustices. Yet leaders have no right to show excessive anger when a follower makes a mistake on a project, misses a deadline, or lacks competence for a particular task. For a leader to remain ethical in their dealings, respect and compassion need to be intact.

Trying to live out the definition of being a person of integrity, 100% of the time, can be extremely problematic to say the least, if we remain in these human bodies. That is why again, I want to be clear that in no way shape or form I am alluding that leaders who demonstrate integrity are operating with moral perfection. I do not believe being perfect is a litmus test for a person operating in integrity. Neither of us are perfect, all leaders make mistakes, and they should not be placed on a pedestal.

There are countless leaders who are known for having integrity and seldom have their motives questioned. They understand that integrity is not a one-time action, but a continuous way of behaving. For leaders seeking to *Raise the BAR: Building Authentic Relationships*, integrity must become a high priority. After all, your integrity is really all that you have. Your words and your actions are your bond. When leaders are not operating in integrity they cannot function as an authentic leader nor can they have authentic relationships.

Loyalty

"Lots of people want to ride with you in the limo, but what you want is someone who will take the bus with you when the limo breaks down."

— Oprah Winfrey

As a recap to the "A Cast of Characters," the main traits leaders need to build and maintain authentic relationships is trust, integrity and loyalty. We've spent a great deal on integrity as it is the crux of the rise and fall of a leader. Now it's time to discuss loyalty. One of the gold standards for any committed relationship is loyalty. Loyalty is defined as "1. Steadfast in allegiance to one's homeland, government, or sovereign, 2. Faithful to a person, ideal, or custom, syn. Faithful, true, constant, steadfast, staunch, resolved, devoted, trustworthy."[73] As seen in the definition, there is honesty and trust, which provides an overlap to this trait. Over time, loyalty will bring mutual interests into shared goals to the point where individuals are committed to give up something of tangible or intangible value to ensure their relationships are bolstered.

Most leaders have a basic understanding of loyalty and how it can foster strong personal and effective relationships. However, what most leaders may not know is that there are at least two components in understanding loyalty that are noteworthy and can have a major impact on how authentic leaders build and sustain their relationships. The first component to understanding loyalty is embracing mutuality and reciprocity as part of the relationships. When individuals develop loyal relationships they are willing to allow their own interests to take a back seat to a person or a cause that is bigger than themselves. This may trigger the need for major sacrifices of time and energy but if you are loyal, you are committed and it is par for the course. Authentic loyalty can require both sides to give something up. Like trust, loyalty is a two-sided coin.

My research demonstrated that mutual and reciprocal relationships are observed in transformational leaders. In Mary Miller's article, "Transformational Leadership and Mutuality," Miller makes the point, "Transformational leadership was conceived by Robert Burns as leaders valued a learning process, specifically leaders who are able to learn from others. The fact that leaders seek to receive from their followers, in Burns' definition, profiles the transformational leaders as learned, not the one who has all the answers. [74] In a sense there is a give and take process that occurs.

The point on mutual and reciprocal relationships can be advanced further when it comes to individuals who seek to be loyal in their working relationships. Ted Engstrom shares in the book, *The Making of a Leader: How to Develop Management and Human Relationship Skills*, "loyalty is expressed in constancy, steadfastness, and faithfulness. A lack of loyalty in leadership can destroy an organization. As the group must be loyal to the leader, the leader in turn must be loyal to the individuals on the team. [75] If an employer wants the employee to be loyal there must visible and clear examples of employer loyalty as well. If employers are not loyal, skilled employees have options to work elsewhere.

Generational Loyalty Differences

All too often relationships with leaders and followers are one-sided due to the fact of superiority over another. This was more evident with Baby Boomers born between 1946 and 1964, yet today Millennials born between 1981-1996 feel empowered to speak up and let their voices and opinions be heard. [76] For loyalty to be authentic the Millennials believe loyalty must flow in both directions. There must be a quid pro quo type of relationship. If no such effort exists and sacrifices are not reciprocated to strengthen the relationship by both parties, then you will have no loyalty or a false sense of loyalty.

For many in today's workforce, the basis of loyalty is a feeling resulting from an established bond that intertwines one person with another. Therein you have a realistic expectation of loyalty and not a blind loyalty, which is false and cannot produce an authentic relationship. Perhaps that is why studies are showing that more than half of today's workforce are in continuous job search mode looking for what they perceive to be better opportunities.

To expand this concept of mutual and reciprocal loyalty from a consumer-based perspective, let me share a few more observations. It appears that the older generations had a fixed brand loyalty more so because of what they learned from their parents. It comes out of maternal influences in their formative years. For example, like wanting to obtain or at minimum drive the "Cutlass Sedan," Oldsmobile like their father. It was the Oldsmobile that exemplified achievement and success for a generation. Now, I know I will lose some, on this point because of the generation gap. Nonetheless, countless "Baby Bloomers" would die to have the vintage Old's with rumble seats.

Oldsmobile was a strongly defined brand. It was Ransom E. Olds, not Henry Ford that put the brand on the map. Believe it or not it was Flavor Flav of the rap group Public Enemy, that declared the "98 Oldsmobile, the ultimate homeboy car." It was a wave of nostalgia that sent the message' "You've got to get Yours" to follow in your father's footsteps. The point here is there was a generation of Oldsmobile loyalists. On somewhat of a somber note, nothing lasts forever. Brands come and go so they must make a strong impact before the competition steers their customers away. Just look at the shift from Cadillacs to Lexus and BMWs, Windows to Macs. Just like brands come and go, people come and go for many reasons that are not always negative. Therefore, leaders should not lose sight of the approaching new and emerging leaders that are coming on the scene. Make room for them, despite them not buying into traditional ways of doing things. While "new" is not always better, the same is true that old is not always the best route either.

Many Millennials take on the posture of "what have you done for me lately?" This becomes true especially in their institutional affiliations and long-and short-term associations. They are willing to give many consumer brands a try until the brand does something that goes against the Millennial's values. Loyalty is important to Millennials and they hold dear to their heart where they place their loyalty. Nevertheless, when it comes to workplace loyalty, Millennials don't view it as valuable as earlier generations. Today, the question that is frequently being asked is, "How is this working for you?" Meaning is this work relationship consequential or challenging, or does it fit in with your goals and purpose? Depending on the answer to the question, there is a thin line between those who remain and those who pursue other goals.

Being loyal to an employer is more complicated than it has ever been before. Why, because individuals' lives are full of twists and turns in this fast paced society. People are prone to shop around than to just stay around. This is especially true as the reality of our economy is ever changing. Bruce Winton, Dean of the Department of Leadership at Regent University, wrote *Be a Leader for God's Sake.* In his book he writes, "Employees today do not see the employer through the same loyalty-shaded glasses, as did the employees of the 1950s. Rather, there is a much greater sense from employees that they stay with an employer because it is mutually beneficial on several levels: in physical terms, such a compensation, in mental terms, such as in stimulating relationships; and in spiritual terms, such that the greater "self" is served and blessed by the involvement with the leader. [77]

There is no getting around the fact that Millennials are here to make their mark on society. Currently, Millennials make up one third of the American workforce, the largest generation at work. [78] By 2020 they will make up 50% of the U.S. workforce. Therefore, leaders may need to rethink and get a better assessment of this group before jumping to conclusions as to how they gage their loyalty since they will likely be a part of the workforce, for the next thirty years. Now, it is true, much of the latest research on Millennials reveals some positive and some negative stereotypes on their behaviors, so it is important to determine what matters most to you.

Positives stereotypes:

- High producers when on the right bus and in the right seat.
- They quantify their work by accomplishments/results not by hours logged. They are willing to labor above and beyond regular hours when it is essential to completing the tasks, but they feel it is pointless to do it habitually.
- Often willing to take risks, where innovative ideas are produced.
- Early adopters to new technology.
- Prone to seek flexible schedule, want the ability to work from anywhere with accountability.
- They want one on one time with the boss from time to time demonstrating the boss cares and is focused on their career too.
- They want to know the "Why" behind everything associated with them. Not afraid to give voice to their concerns.
- Dress code are not important, implied originality.

- **Negatives Stereotypes:**
- They are narcissistic (self-absorbed)
- Disloyal
- Can't interact face to face
- Lethargic
- Seeks privilege
- High maintenance.
- Not afraid to relocate from job to job, if it does not fit. Millennials switch jobs every 26 months.

Loyalty and Longevity

The second component of loyalty is being able to differentiate between longevity and loyalty. In the workforce there appears to be a "romance loyalty" with prolonged existence of no real growth or responsibilities. This leads to the crux of the matter in getting past the superficial aspects of loyalty to explore beyond the surface to find out whether someone is loyal or are they staying with the company for the benefits that are provided in the relationships. Too many "Baby Boomers" stayed in positions for fear of change or taking risks, apathy, or having no other alternatives. In some cases, money could have been an incentive, but it is not always the case. People should not be baited like animals waving carrot sticks.

Just because someone is working alongside an individual for a long period of time does not mean they are loyal. In authentic relationships it is vital to identify people who are loyal and not just longstanding. In all relationships according to Kouser and Posner, "loyalty is not something a boss can demand. It is something the people—the team—chooses to grant to a leader who has earned it. The employee's choice is based not upon authority, but upon the leader's perceived capacity to serve a need. [79] In today's work culture there are many needs that surface, in that it is difficult for the leader to pin-point the wishes of their employees as it relates to being loyal. In Gary Chapman's *The Five Love Languages*, leaders may need to assess their followers, "loyalty language" in order to build and sustain working relationships. Leaders should make an effort to find out what makes an employee want to hang around or take flight. Loyalty to an organization or a person today is based more on people feeling like they are a part of something; a sense of belonging, not just a number on a status report. Remember this is not your father's Oldsmobile!

While many organizations give generous perks to their employees, perks alone may not create loyalty. Now may be the time for leaders to reconsider loyalty in their relationships from both sides of the fence. Since we see that the traditional methods and models of loyalty are not the most beneficial, particularly if it is based on time in a position then more conversation needs to be discussed. In many corporate settings, reconsidering loyalty is not a foreign idea. Companies are no longer only building loyalty around time, money and rewards points alone. They are seeking to build loyalty among relationships and unforgettable experiences.

I attended a farewell celebration for an employee who had been with the organization for what appeared to be a short amount of time. Many even referred to the person as a "short-timer." Much to my surprise, despite the fact that this employee was leaving, many of the co-workers shared passionately how much they learned from the employee, how new ideas were on the table, and the employees better approach to doing traditional things. The lesson learned is that leaders must be careful not to miss the value of the experience versus focusing on the time of the experience. One of my favorite lines from the movie *Steel Magnolias* is when Julia Roberts character said, "I would rather have thirty minutes of something wonderful than a lifetime of nothing special."

More and more employers are building loyalty through balanced relationships as opposed to duration, that speaks to respecting the employees' competencies and skill sets. Leaders respect employees by empowering them to make decisions and allowing employees the freedom to take initiative and do things without being told. Also, respect is a two-way street, so both leaders and followers should show their respect by respecting themselves.

Leaders are not necessarily the one to fix all the problems. There should not be an expectation that a leader is superman or superwoman. People will willingly follow the direction of someone who is attuned to their aspirations, fears, and ideals. Without strong internal loyalty among the leaders and followers in our churches and workplaces, it's nearly impossible to generate authentic loyalty. Remember, the primary goal is to have a team that is both longstanding and loyal.

When you look at companies like Starbucks, Southwest Airlines, and Chick-fil-A, they attract loyal customers and loyal employees because of a positive experience that management ensures is provided. These companies are not just product-friendly, they go out of their way to be people-friendly. These companies provide an experience that adds to the individuals by showing them they play a significant role in the establishment through an emotional connection. Leaders who can express passion and participate with their employees in the overall goals of the organization are often able to succeed in building loyal connections.

"I've learned that people will forget what you said,
people will forget what you did, but people
will never forget how you made them feel."

— Dr. Maya Angelou

In simple terms, it is about the individual's feelings from the experience of being inspired by their leaders. In a society that seems to be moving away from touchy-feely experiences, I believe there are more people than not that relish in feeling appreciated and esteemed. In the long run it will create deeper connections. How leaders make people feel in a healthy sense never goes out of style. With that being said, companies are going beyond the transactional (monetary motivations) experience, or you give me 30 years of service and I will give you a gold watch because these incentives don't work today.

Using loyalty as the gold standard for measuring the quality of connections with people who want to build solid and enduring relationships is key. True loyalty will stand the test of time. Looking at the big picture when defining loyalty, the question that needs to be asked is, Does it rank high on the leadership scale in our churches and workplaces? Anything that value is not placed on, will in the end be devalued. As with every type of relationship rarely does the process of building and sustaining it follow in a straight line. There will always be ebbs and flows, twist and turns because of the uniqueness of our individuality.

Therefore, it can be expected that there will be complex challenges to overcome our differences in how we find solutions to our dilemmas. In loyalty relationships there will always be a need for individuals to have empathy, be flexible, willing to compromise, (not your values) and moving from the mind-set that this is the way we have always done it. Fostering loyal relationships will cause leaders to move into unoccupied territory where a "new normal" can take place. "Do not conform to the pattern of this world but be transformed by the renewing of your mind. Then you will be able to test and approve what God's will is – his good, pleasing and perfect will." [80]

A final thought on loyalty is that traditional loyalty is becoming obsolete in our workforces and church cultures. However, I would say that leaders need to have the foresight to see loyalty in a transformative way in order to maximize productivity (not just the bottom line) as they interact with those in their organizations to increase loyalty from different perspectives. Understanding the difference between longevity and loyalty are essential to change the end game of advancing a culture of loyal relationships.

Chapter 9: Part II - Cast of Characters

Ethical and Unethical Behaviors

1. Many leaders have a sense of entitlement and believe that they should be allowed to cut corners or bend the rules to their benefit. Share your thoughts.

2. Unethical behavior by leaders can damage the credibility of the organization. What tools (policies, procedures, resources) does your organization use to ensure ethical behavior is maintained?

3. Organizations don't make decisions—people do. How have you handled ethical dilemmas in your organization? How did loyalty play in your decision?

4. Not all ethical challenges have a clear right/wrong answer. As a leader, what can you do or who do you turn to for advice with the "gray areas."

____

____

____

____

5. Why do you think we continue to see so many scandals among our leaders in the public arena? What have you learned from past scandals?

____

____

____

____

PART VI

Emotional Intelligence (EI)

"My psychiatrist says a few more sessions and I'll be able to get my emotional baggage into a carry-on."

CHAPTER 10

The Game Changer - Emotional Intelligence (EI)

"We live our lives through our emotions, and it is our emotions that give our lives meaning. What interests or fascinates us, who we love, what angers us, what bores us—all of this defines us. Gives us character and constitutes who we are."
— ***Robert Solomon***

In writing this chapter, I do so with full disclosure. I admit that my understanding of Emotional Intelligence (EI), was severely lacking before I engaged in this subject matter during extensive research for my doctoral dissertation. What stood out for me after interviewing 10 senior pastors on several subjects, ranging from what it means to be authentic, to an understanding of EI, I discovered that only one of the ten pastors displayed any sense or awareness of EI.

EI for Church Leaders

The questionnaire I used to measure the EI of the pastors, was the same tool I used to gauge my own level of EI. It was then that I realized that I also had blood on my hands in how I unknowingly was operating as a leader without consciousness of my EI. It was clear that my EI ranked alongside the other nine Senior Pastors. Thus, there was no way I could pass judgment on what appeared to be another pastor's lack of awareness on this important subject.

Our role as leaders in the church is to develop disciples spiritually, which is only the tip of the iceberg. Little attention is being paid to the discipleship of people to become emotionally mature. A person's maturity is beneath the surface. I believe leaders need to find a balance between the spiritual and emotional side of their behaviors to produce long-lasting positive outcomes. Balance is truly the key to success as one should not be weightier than the other so that you do not become blind-sided in one area. Feelings and facts are needed to make sound decisions, and sometimes showing frustration with a situation is OK as it will get your team's attention to the seriousness of the matter.

Parenthetically speaking from the church perspective, many leaders are frequently blamed for the problems their follower's encounter. Leaders are targeted with a lot of bumps and bruises for things that are beyond their control. Followers must take personal responsibility for their behavior just as a leader should. The challenge is that a leader is in essence a brand for his church. Therefore, anything the leader does personally is a reflection of the church. On the other hand, anything a church follower does, is a reflection on the leader. There should be more of a delineation however society does not view it that way even if followers don't adhere to the leader's teachings. I believe much of the blame stems from people being inflicted with a great deal of baggage and hurt from those in a position of leadership and trust, and they never heal.

In *The Emotionally Healthy Church; A Strategy for Discipleship that Actually Changes Lives,* Peter Scazzero lists twelve factors that can help us grow our EI:

"i) Naming, recognizing, and managing our own feelings;
ii) identifying and having active compassion for others;
iii) initiating and maintaining close and meaningful relationships;
iv) breaking free from self-destructive patterns;
v) being aware of how our past impacts our present;
vi) developing the capacity to express our thoughts and feelings clearly, both verbally and nonverbally;
vii) respecting and loving others without having to change them;
viii) asking what we need, want, or prefer clearly, directly and respectfully;
ix) accurately self-assessing our strengths, limits and weaknesses and freely sharing them with others;
x) learning the capacity to resolve conflict maturely and negotiate solutions that consider the perspective of others;
xi) distinguishing and appropriately expressing our sexuality and sensuality; and xii) grieving well. [81]"

All of the twelve tasks mentioned above require an authentic self-evaluation. In addition, in another one of Scazzero's books, *The Emotionally Healthy Church,* he makes it abundantly clear that, "it is not possible for a Christian to be spiritually mature while remaining emotionally immature."[82] When leaders and followers do not mature optimally, they drag excess baggage from their childhood and adolescence years into their leadership behavior, and make decisions not based on the true anointing of the Holy spirit. It's been said that if the leader and follower are not careful, they can allow their past to blackmail their future. As you know, years of psychological research confirms that our family origin and genetics can have significant impact on how our lives are shaped and how we have been influenced. Both leaders and followers must be willing to examine their past to unload the excess emotional baggage to function effectively. Leaders need to find ways to lighten their load and intentionally engage in healthier behaviors and activities. A few things leaders can do include:

- Blocking out time on your calendar to engage in healthy activities such as exercise, eating better, or going out for fun with friends and family.
- Make personal time for reflection and unwinding (this is separate from studying for sermon).
- Delegate unnecessary tasks.
- Travel more and take in the sights to enjoy the moment.
- Encourage team members to follow your "me time" routine and make it a priority.

Using EI as a self-awareness tool can truly enhance your leadership abilities. It will make you more aware of your strengths and weaknesses and keep you in check-up mode of how you are interacting with others. You will become more in tune with your emotions and learn when to exercise self-control, offer praise, or receive feedback in any environment. Out of everything discussed in this book, EI will become the Game Changer to your success in *Building Authentic Relationships*.

EI in the Workplace

The reality is that leaders are filled with emotion-generating events daily. While most leaders come into leadership roles understanding their responsibilities to move the organization ahead but they fail to take a serious assessment to manage their emotions in the heat of challenging problems including failing to meet goals, employee retention and satisfaction, and other management crises. For the most part, the skills needed in managing one's emotions were not taught in colleges and universities, seminaries, or conventional work environments, until a couple decades ago and understanding one's emotions were not a part of essential training to be a successful leader.

However, in the 90's Peter Salovey and John Mayer introduced the term Emotional Intelligence (EI), arguing that leaders' emotional reactions to events have a significant effect on their attitudes and behaviors. Since that time, EI has risen to a higher level of priority in forecasting the achievement of the leader more so than his Intelligence Quotient (IQ). Tons of research revealed that EI is an extremely important skill for personal and professional success as leaders work through obstacles in the workplace and beyond.

Since we are all human, during our waking moments we are constantly responding to our emotions based on personal experiences and what is going on around us. To make it plain, your emotions are your feelings. Therefore, it is critical for leaders to learn to pay attention to their positive and negative reactions as they work through the ups and downs on any given day to maintain a healthy emotional climate. Why? Because much is determined through the leader's and his team's EI that will forecast their effectiveness and the growth of the organization, as well as bring out the best in leaders and the followers.

"Self-aware leaders are tuned to their inner signals. If a person is perpetually oblivious to his own feelings, he will tune out how others feel."

— Daniel Goleman

As I was gaining a working understanding of EI, I reflected on my days working in the government sector. After receiving a promotion, I was charged with the supervision of 15 people whom I worked alongside for many years. The transition of becoming the supervisor of your peers was drama in itself. I knew them and they knew me. My focus was always on the technical aptitude or certain specific expertise of my employees. I never gave a second thought to what was playing out in their emotions as well as my own. Even though there was always lots of backbiting, complaints, and at times immature behavior, I was more concerned with the performance of my team and how it would reflect on *me* as a new supervisor, and not what was driving the emotional atmosphere. I did not realize that my lack of emotional intelligence and that of my subordinates that was playing out in our everyday lives by exhibiting some of the behaviors below. Refer back to this list as your Emotional Checklist to work on these negative characteristics to change your body language and communication in leading others:

1. Talking down to people
2. Fault-finding
3. Nitpicking,
4. Giving short answers
5. Belittling
6. Being disrespectful to others time
7. Never willing to say I was wrong
8. Never willing to say I made a mistake
9. Short-sighted
10. Short-fused
11. Demeaning
12. Being self-protective
13. Quick-tempered

14. Standoffish
15. Having a sense of entitlement
16. Feeling vulnerable
17. Anxious
18. Narcissistic
19. Abusing power
20. Disregard for morale
21. Being rude
22. Bullying
23. Not valuing others opinions
24. Lack of empathy
25. Passive-Aggressive

Do any of these sound familiar? Do you see yourself or your superior's behavior in the list above? Now, I am clear most leaders do not intentionally make it a habit to start their day with personal vendettas to mistreat, disvalue, or abuse, those on their team, but unfortunately this happens often. I've found that much of the behavior from those who lack EI is produced from frustration, anxiety, and stress that creeps into the challenges every leader faces daily become par for the course.

Leaders have to make a deliberate choice to be mindful of their emotional health. Not once did I make the connection that *my* unpredictable moods and behaviors were playing a major part in the lack of EI on my team. As a leader, I was disconnected and my team felt I was out of touch with their reality. I was shocked when my team members told me that they had to brace themselves to ask me a question or voice their opinion as they were afraid of what mood I was in that day. More importantly, I did not realize that moods can be contagious for better or worse.

What has become even more apparent to me after almost eight years of observing and doing significant research on this subject is the damaging impact this negative behavior is having in today's workforce. We are witnessing the lack of EI at the highest levels of government, corporate America, and religious institutions. As a result of my own EI assessment on the topic, I realized that EI, is a learned behavior that can be cultivated over time in everyone. Therefore, I was challenged to put some guardrails in place and paid attention to my emotions and that of others.

In order for me to become more effective in my leadership, one of the first things I did was recited this prayer often: "*Search me, O God and know my heart, Try me, and know my anxieties, and see if there is any wicked way in me, and lead me in the way everlasting*" Psalm 139:23-24. In addition to praying, I made intentional efforts to incorporate the following behaviors as I interacted with my team and colleagues. I considered these new behaviors my "*Game Changer,*" so at the end of the day my goal was to decrease the negative impact I personally had on my team.

1. "***Reflection.***" Reflection starts with monitoring and defining what you are feeling over a period of time. Reflecting is like looking in the mirror, examining all of the warts, blemishes and making a decision to see a demonologist to fix the problem, however it must be both an inward change as well as outward change. As I began reflecting, I asked myself, what could I have done or said differently to make the outcome go in a positive direction? What prompted my behavior to act negatively? What

was my underlying issue? Reflecting takes time which required me to go through periods of solitude. We live in a society that wants instant responses; like a microwave rather than a slow cooker. Reflecting must be high on the leader's list of things to do to reap a major ROI (return on their investment) with their team.

2. ***"Feedback."*** There are two sides to the spectrum when it comes to feedback: giving and receiving. Giving feedback does not always have to be negative, even if it is not what the person wants to hear. After reflecting, when I began providing feedback, I was careful to do it in a way that the person knew that I was sincere and had their best interest at heart. I did everything possible to convey that I wanted to help them and not harm them. I did so by using the person's name often and thanking them for a specific task. I used the word team often and smiled and nodded in agreement when the person spoke. I've learned that one major reason some leaders shy away from giving feedback is because it is often bad news, and no one wants to be the bearer of bad news.

   Nonetheless, leaders can't bury their heads in the sand and act like nothing ever happened. Team members want feedback when things are going well and not so well. As a cautionary tale to leaders you need to solicit feedback and be open and listen to what is being said. This increases your credibility and helps to build bonds of trust in the relationship. If you don't solicit feedback you can appear as though you know it all and don't make mistakes. The saying goes, "People don't care how much you know until they know how much you care." Make a mental note to give and receive feedback to help build an approachable work atmosphere.

3. ***"Praise."*** Giving praise to others is a prescription for human satisfaction. Look for the good first from those in your sphere of influence. All humans seek to be appreciated and acknowledged for their actions. We all have a need for respect, recognition, and to be esteemed. These emotionally healthy needs fall in line with American psychologist Abraham Maslow's, fifth stage of his well-known hierarchy of human physical needs. When praise in given people feel special. Always find something about the person and offer praise first, even if there is a need for chastisement. Small words of praise may appear to be insignificant, nonetheless, they can have a major effect in building relationships.

These three action steps: Reflect, Feedback and Praise, were the result of me taking courageous steps to come out of my comfort zone to deal with my emotions as I engaged others. I needed a paradigm shift so that I could experience real transformation in my EI self-awareness. As it states in Romans 12:2 "*And do not be conformed to this world, but be transformed by the renewing of your mind, that you may prove what is that good and acceptable and perfect will of God.*" I actually saw a transformation of my heart and mind when I gave equal weight to my spiritual and emotional development. This is not an easy process and it takes practice and commitment. I certainly know that I have not arrived and have work to do.

It was actually during one of my "*aha*" moments, that I learned I needed more direction, insight, and guidance into this EI response. I was in search of my yellow brick road, after all, I realized I was not in Kansas (the government sector) anymore. The stakes were higher and the losses would be too great if I did not yield to understanding what was going inside of me first. We all have experienced some form of pain, disappointment, and failure in our lives. So how do we balance our personal frustrations while leading? What have we learned from these experiences that has helped build our character? What will it take for us to be mature enough to let it go and not carry it around like a monkey on our backs? Throughout Scripture the Apostle Paul shows us that during his weakest moments he understood what it meant to depend on God alone. Paul's revelation became his Game Changer in his walk with God. So far, what has been your leadership Game Changer?

Ultimately, we are all a work in progress, especially if we are willing to have the conversations and take it one day at a time in improving our EI. Leaders can take "Action Steps" to move forward but they can also take steps back when they realize they have made some mistakes. Mistakes are learning opportunities. If you made an unhealthy decision for your team or had a total lapse in judgment, you should quickly admit it and take steps to demonstrate your shift. Bad decisions can cast a dark shadow on the leader's credibility, even though few in your organization will speak about it publicity, they are talking about it in the parking lot and at the water cooler. Like the Emperor without any clothes, everyone is aware of it so act quickly to change the mindset.

Since no man or woman is an island, relationships are an essential and a fulfilling part of life. Every leader is only half of the relationship, so he or she must own their half and take the responsibility to understand the critical need to enhance their emotional intelligence skills. When leaders are aware of their emotional intelligence, they are also aware of the emotional intelligence of those they serve, which ultimately leads to better outcomes for everyone involved.

EI From the Experts

> *"Emotional intelligence is your ability to recognize and understand emotions in yourself and others, and your ability to use this awareness to manage your behavior and relationships. Emotional intelligence is the "something" in each of us that is a bit intangible. It affects how we manage behavior, navigate social complexities, and make personal decisions that achieve positive results."* [83]

Authors Travis Bradberry and Jean Greaves offer an easy to understand practical guide to emotional intelligence in their book, *Emotional Intelligence 2.0*. They break down four emotional intelligence skills under two primary competencies: i) personal competence; and ii) social competence.

Personal competence:

- **Self-Awareness skills** – is the leader's ability to accurately perceive their own emotions in the moment and understand their tendencies across situations. It includes the leader staying on top of evolving situations and their typical reactions to specific events, challenges, and people. With a keen understanding, the leader can make sense of his emotions. Self-aware leaders spend time thinking through where the emotions are coming from and why they are occurring. Emotions always serve a purpose because they are the leaders reaction to the world around them.
- **Self-management skills** - when the leader acts—or does not act. It is her ability to use her self-awareness to stay flexible and direct her behavior positively. Some emotions create a paralyzing fear that can cloud thinking, yet once the leader understands

and builds comfort with her feelings, the best course of action will show itself and be the obvious choice.

Social competence:

- **Social awareness skills:** your ability to accurately pick up on emotions in other people and understand what is really going on with them. This can mean perceiving what other people are thinking and feeling even if you do not feel the same way. It's easy to get caught in your own emotions and forget to consider the feelings of the other party. Social awareness requires you to stay focused and absorb critical information. Listening and observing are the most important elements of social awareness. Therefore, be mindful to stop talking and stop anticipating what the other person might say next. This takes a lot of practice as you are processing people's emotions in the actual moment, as you are a contributing member of the interaction.
- **Relationship management skills:** is your ability to use your self-awareness of your own emotions and the emotions of others to oversee positive connections among leaders and followers. It is about building relationships that require an investment of time. Using your relationship skill does not necessarily mean these people become your BFF (Best Friends for Forever) but it does mean that there is respect and the lines of communication are open to reduce conflict.

"If a person can't effectively lead his own life and control himself, how should he be expected to provide effective leadership to others?"

— Samuel D. Rima

This point is further explored in the book, *Primal Leadership: Learning to Lead with Emotional Intelligence* by Daniel Goleman who points out that emotions are contagious. He believes that a leader's first task is to get his own emotions in check like good hygiene. [84]

> "Authentic leaders experience more positive emotions as a result of greater self-awareness. Their positive attitudes and behavior will, in turn, be carried over to their followers through both behavioral modeling and emotional contagion processes." [85]

As you may be aware, there have been a number of social experiments to demonstrate that acts of kindness are contagious. This topic has also been discussed in what has been called positive psychology. When leaders go out of their way to help team members in good times or in a time of crisis, their actions create a lasting positive impression on those who follow. More importantly, companies have found that when employees receive discounts or free branded products from their employer it results in higher employee satisfaction and increased productivity as employees had more pride in their work at the company. When people are exposed to kindness and generosity, they are more likely to pay it forward. Positivity begets positivity. Go ahead, try it!

EI in the Bible

Although the term EI did not come into existence until the 90s, the required skill sets were being used and developed by leaders in Scripture. EI comes to mind when Paul told Timothy "To keep a close watch on yourself and on your teaching. Persist in this, for by so doing, you will save both yourself and your hearers." (1 Tim 4:16). Basically Paul was instructing Timothy on self-awareness and self-control. Paul's advice has a deeper meaning in that he wants Timothy to be aware of his actions, tone, interactions with others and his statements. As a Christian leader Timothy is a reflection of Christ and His Word and if he faithfully abides by the Word he will be saved and so will those who hear his message. Therefore, as leaders we should heed Paul's advice and be cognizant of our actions, emotions, and words.

Throughout the Old and New Testaments, as well as in the Psalms, we see snapshots of how EI played a major role as to whether God's leaders were successful in carrying out their assignments. God himself expressed a variety of emotions in several places in the Hebrew text. God was grieved at the sinfulness of His creation, "And the Lord was sorry that He had made man on the earth, He grieved in His heart" (Genesis 6:4); He was angered at their idolatry (Jer 2:11-13); "They provoked him to jealousy with foreign gods; with abomination, they provoked Him to angered" (Deut 32:16). The Lord shows "compassion" and remembers that we "are but dust" (Ps 103:13-14).

In the honesty of the Scriptures we can see that when emotions are not put under control they can lead to obsessions. This can be seen in the life of King Saul and his foolish "Rash Oath" (1 Samuel 14:23), after he was rejected as king and became depressed and wanted to kill David. The Spirit of the Lord departed from Saul and a distressing spirit from the Lord troubled him" (1 Samuel 16:14). This distressing spirit would be understood as depression. Saul became depressed and anxiety built up in his heart. "Anxiety in the heart of man causes depression (Proverbs 12:25). Then we see David's obsessive, lustful relationship with Bathsheba (2 Samuel 11:1-17). David's lust led to the killing of Uriah, Bathsheba's husband (2 Samuel 11:15). Through all of David's challenges, he grieved by writing songs and poems before he inherited the throne.

There were numerous emotions expressed in the Psalms, the book of Jeremiah and Lamentations as laments went up to God. The book of Psalms reflects the entire range of human emotions. We see a loving

God demonstrating how a shepherd cares for his sheep and remain peaceful in difficult times (Psalms 23). The entire book explores the ups and downs of a David, a great leader's humanity.

Jeremiah, who was called the "weeping prophet," dealt with fear, despair, joy and praise. He cried out, "O my soul, my soul! I am pained in my very heart! My heart makes a noise in me, I cannot hold my peace." (Jeremiah 4:19) As Jeremiah dealt with conflicting emotions he turned to God to receive encouragement. As leaders deal with their emotions they should always seek God first and then to others. The very act of showing one another empathy leads to sustainable emotional health. Jeremiah teaches leaders that in the midst of emotional despair, taking a moment to reflect on the situation can prove to be a way of escape. This can move the needle towards better emotional health.

Some the most poignant expressions of emotions are found in the New Testament in the life of Jesus. Jesus expressed compassion for the hungry (Matthew 15:32, 20:34); Jesus felt grief at the death of His friend Lazarus (John 11:35); and He wept over Jerusalem because the people did not recognize His presence (Luke 19:41-44). Then we are told about two incidents just before His death where Jesus experienced great sorrow and abandonment. In the Garden of Gethsemane Jesus said to his disciples "My soul is exceedingly sorrowful, even to death. Stay here and watch with me (Matthew 26:38). As Jesus neared his death He recognized the need to be in relationship with the disciples and not isolate himself. Therefore, as leaders manage their emotions, key relationships are needed and withdrawal from people can often add more stress to the situation. As He hung on the cross, Jesus cried out with a loud voice, "My God, My God why have you forsaken me?" (Matthew 27:46). Feelings of abandonment are often typical experiences of leaders who are not managing their emotions correctly. Such a disconnect to the team can cause great leaders to look for connections in unhealthy environments and behaviors.

The Bible helps us to understand that what goes on in the mind comes out in actions, positive or negative. Emotions are at the core of our being reflecting our attitudes and behavior. Emotions are a gift from God intended to compel us to act in one form or another. However, the challenge comes when our emotions control us rather than us controlling them. No emotion was intended to cause hurt or result in manipulation of other people. God never intended that His creation be ruled by their emotions. When Jesus referred to the abundant life, He described a life in balance where our emotions are under control.[86].

Eventually, most of the dysfunction around unmanaged emotions will dissipate when leaders acknowledge their dependence on God and seek support, encouragement and accountability from those they trust. Iron sharpens iron. There also must be a commitment to do the hard work to reap the benefits of being an emotionally healthy leader. In the end, when leaders get a grip on their EI and are willing to seek change in areas they are deficient, true transformation will take place. EI self-awareness will become the real Game Changer in the way leaders think about their emotions and behavior towards others in *Building* valuable *Authentic Relationships.*

Chapter 10: The Game Changer: Emotional Intelligence (EI)

1. A key characteristic of leaders operating with EI is self-awareness. Are you usually aware of your feelings? Do you know your blind spots? How do you react to criticism?

2. Social and cultural awareness are critical for people operating with a high EI. Describe how you deal with a difficult person in your environment. What steps do you take to work with that person?

3. As a leader, what is your main focus on a typical day: tasks and results or people and emotions? Explain.

4. Are you adaptable to change? How would you react if you were told a project you've worked on for six months will shut down for something better?

____

____

____

____

5. What would you do if a team member told you that they felt they were being treated unfairly?

____

____

____

____

CHAPTER 11

Baggage Check

When it comes to being authentic,
either you are striving or you are not.

All leaders come to the table with some unintended baggage. If they continue to carry that baggage it will keep them from being their authentic selves. Leaders tap into their authentic selves by first being honest and acknowledging their flaws. Authenticity does not equate to perfection. When leaders are not willing to unpack, sort through, or lighten their baggage, they end up transporting their past into their future. If that means leaders engaging in therapy to resolve childhood pain, brokenness in relationships and emotional setbacks, then that should be the beginning of their journey. If internal baggage continues unchecked, these leaders end up bleeding over everyone in their sphere of influence. Studies show that what happened to an individual at age five, can affect them and others at age fifty-five, if not properly dealt with and exposed. Seeking help to become your best authentic self is a key sign of growth.

We All Fall Short

Being Authentic is the ability to reveal one's strengths, weaknesses and effectively utilize them as opportunities to be successful. Realizing that for leader's honesty (especially for those who are Christians) comes into play when leaders are willing to admit they are redeemed sinners who still have struggles.[87]

All leaders have flaws, make mistakes, and miss the mark from time to time. However, authentic leaders do more than learn from their experiences. We often hear the phrase "experience is the best teacher." I would argue the point that experience may not necessarily be the best teacher. One of my professors at Regent University shared with the class "It is reflecting on those experiences that the lessons of life are learned." In essence, what she was saying is that you may have experience in dealing with a situation, but it is not until you take the time to reflect on the experience by pondering what went right, and what went wrong, is when the lesson becomes clearer.

Especially if there was some pain and sorrow involved in the experience. Pain helps us to know something is wrong and there is a need for correction. Authentic leaders use their pain to help them to move from pain to purpose. Reflections take time and honesty. Reflections will cause you to strongly consider how you would handle this situation the next time. "Reflection time is like meditation time." Authentic leaders who reflect, learn from their mistakes, whereas inauthentic leaders react from their mistakes.

It was Socrates that said: "The unexamined life is not worth living."

The reality is that no leader should announce "I am authentic!" If they do, at that moment, any semblance of authenticity ceases. Authenticity cannot be manufactured or manipulated. It is just like saying to someone "I am humble." Humility and authenticity are attributes that leaders cannot assign to themselves—it's your actions that will shine through and others will utter those words about you. When it comes to being authentic, either you are striving to be or you are not.

Inauthentic Leaders

To the contrary, the case must be made that inauthentic leadership can be summed up as those with unbridled self-interests that motivate some leaders to treat people as a means to their own end. The truth is, sometimes authenticity does not always have positive connotations. Sometimes a leader's actions lead them to a dark, self-serving lifestyle. Unfortunately, these leaders never defeated their inner demons, which in due course leads to their demise. While it is true that most leaders will not become mass murderers, however, as a cautionary tale, there is always a need for all leaders to check themselves and their baggage in addition to having people in their lives to hold them accountable. That is why the Scriptures remind us "that the heart is desperately wicked and who can know it."[88] For this reason it is critical that leaders particularly in the church, understand that authenticity is more than being who you are, it is also a matter of being who God created you to be.

Leaders who live inauthentic and operate in pseudo behavior are playing with fire. They often find themselves on a slippery slope, walking on eggshells, always looking over their shoulders, because sooner than later their true character will be exposed in a less than attractive photo on the six o'clock news. Herein is where private behavior collides with public life.

Consequently, amid this dilemma and moral decline, there is a need to rebuild confidence and credibility in our leaders. As well as a need to promote a leadership paradigm that will forge leaders at all levels into behaviors that will elevate the need for honesty, integrity, loyalty, accountability and transparency as the hallmark in the church and the workplace. Thus, the case is being made to encourage leaders to model the tenets of authenticity which lately is in short supply.

Chapter 11: The Baggage Check

1. Write out at least three strengths and weaknesses. Describe steps to improve on your weaknesses.

2. How have you handled distressing emotions lately (i.e. when things don't go as planned)? Do you recover quickly or do you remain stressed? Discuss.

3. Are you in tune with the people's feelings around you and usually understand where they are coming from? Discuss.

4. How adept are you dealing with the emotional baggage of others? Choose at least one: i) Control freak; ii) Constant yeller; iii) Overly dramatic.

____

____

____

____

5. Do you ever find yourself pretending to be who you are not to please others? If so, share in one or two sentences. If you are comfortable being your true self, how did you come to this place?

____

____

____

____

PART VII

The Results Are In!

CHAPTER 12

Are We There Yet?

"If you want to improve the organization, you have to improve yourself and the organization gets pulled up with you."

— Indra Nooyi

The answer to the opening chapter question is best summed up in the previous cartoon, "Actual results may vary." Everything we do on our authentic journey depends upon how diligent we are at staying the course. It starts with how we prepare ourselves each morning, how we manage our time throughout the day, and how we choose to interact in our relationships. We have been on a journey to *Raise the Bar* among leaders in the church and the workplace to encourage them to build authentic relationships with those within the leader's sphere of influence.

Authentic leadership focuses on self-awareness, moral integrity, transparency, empathy, and open and honest communication. It also requires the leader to take a balanced approach in decision-making by seeking input from the team. This type of leadership produces healthy leaders and followers which adds value to any organization. True authentic leadership creates a positive work environment as well as fostering a high follower performance and career advancement.

Another key aspect of authentic leadership is trust. When leaders trust that their team can perform their jobs professionally with minimal direction, it boosts morale and productivity. By the same token, trust is a two-way street, and when employees trust that their leader has their best interest at heart and that their leader is "walking the walk" it builds strong, loyal relationships. In addition, the VAT Principles of Vulnerability, Accountability, and Transparency should be evident and high on the list in exhibiting an authentic leader's qualities.

Since no one knows you like you know yourself, it's best to come to the table with an honest self-awareness of your strengths and weaknesses. Bill George, an authority on authenticity and character-based leadership, stated, "The hardest person you will ever have to lead is yourself." Leaders must make a decision as to whether they want to take their personal growth and development seriously. The viability and success of the organization depends on it.

Let's face it, none of us are perfect, so working to improve intellectually, emotionally, spiritually, morally, and physically can be beneficial to our health and well-being. Leaders can start their authentic journey by being mindful of a few qualities that authentic leaders possess:

i) Admitting to their mistakes;

ii) Apologizing when they are wrong;

iii) Showing empathy;

iv) Listening to their teams ideas and perspectives;

v) Treating everyone fairly;

vi) Being an authentic role model by your words and deeds; and above all

vii) Doing the right thing!

A final point I wanted to make is about our physical bodies. Authentic leadership requires a healthy mindset. A healthy mind and a healthy body function better together. Therefore, prioritizing your physical health is necessary in your transformation. Scripture tells us, "therefore, honor God with your bodies," (1 Corinthians 6:20). Leaders should take into consideration their diet, exercise routine, and ensuring that they get a good night's sleep to help alleviate some of the stress and anxiety that it takes to lead. Our health affects our mood and emotions so our commitment and self-discipline in this area will go a long way for our mental and physical endurance to achieve our desired outcome.

I have provided an Authenticity Roadmap to help you craft your Personal Leadership Development Plan and take into account your Core Values, VAT and P.E.A.C.E characteristics as your guide. Consider long, medium, and short term goals as you are working on your plan. Although the road ahead is challenging as leadership has its highs and lows, success is imminent if you put forth your best effort to change. In the words of leadership expert John Maxwell, "The more seriously you take your growth, the more seriously your people will take you." *Raise the BAR* to a higher authentic leadership standard today.

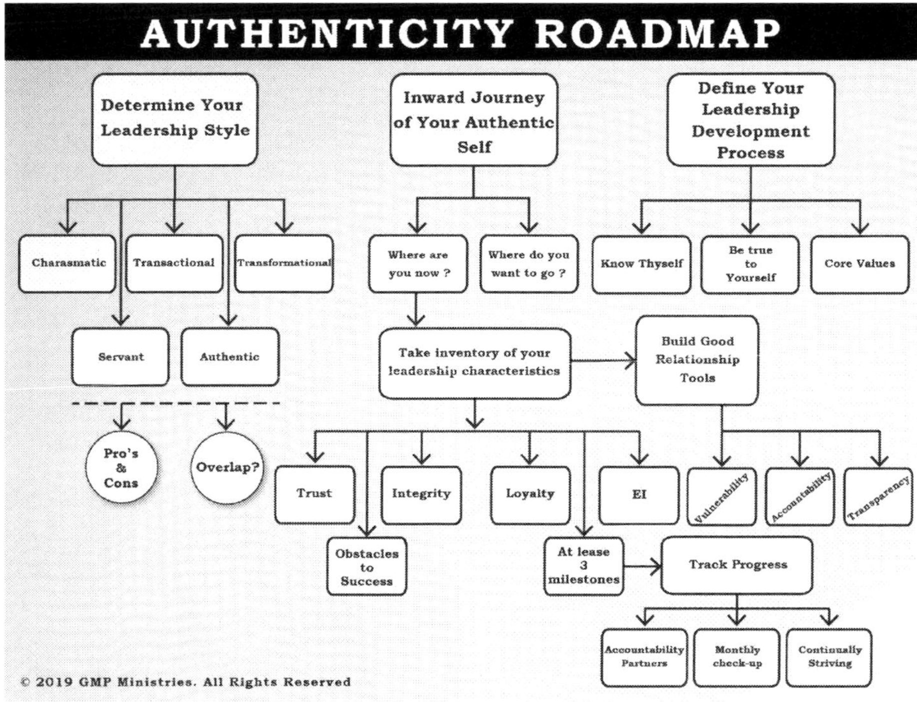
AUTHENTICITY ROADMAP
Determine Your Leadership Style
Inward Journey of Your Authentic Self
Define Your Leadership Development Process
Charasmatic
Transactional
Transformational
Where are you now ?
Where do you want to go ?
Know Thyself
Be true to Yourself
Core Values
Servant
Authentic
Take inventory of your leadership characteristics
Build Good Relationship Tools
Pro's & Cons
Overlap?
Trust
Integrity
Loyalty
EI
Vulnerability
Accountability
Transparency
Obstacles to Success
At lease 3 milestones
Track Progress
Accountability Partners
Monthly check-up
Continually Striving
© 2019 GMP Ministries. All Rights Reserved

Reverend Doctor Gloria Miller Perrin

Bachelor of Arts, Master of Divinity, Doctor of Ministry

The Reverend Dr. Gloria Miller Perrin is a native of Washington, DC. She began her career at the Department of the Navy, and excelled to the management level as a Supervisory Contract Specialist. Dr. Miller Perrin graduated from Trinity College in Washington, DC with a Bachelor of Arts Degree and Howard University in Washington, DC with a Master of Divinity Degree.

Reverend Dr. Miller Perrin was called and licensed to preach the Gospel at the Peoples Church in Washington, DC. She was ordained and served as Assistant Pastor at the Saint Paul Baptist Church in Capitol Heights, Maryland for thirteen years. Among her varying assignments, she was also responsible for the Women's Ministry and the Rites of Passage Ministry for young girls. Reverend Dr. Miller Perrin served as the first Protestant Chaplain for Trinity College and provided consultant services for the Women's Ministry at Bronx Christian Fellowship Church located in the Bronx, New York.

Reverend Dr. Miller Perrin is a distinguished preacher, teacher, and ecumenical retreat consultant, specializing in Social Justice and Women's Issues. She is noted for political activity and her ability to develop partnerships between the church and community to understand the relationship of spiritual development and social concerns. Reverend Dr. Miller Perrin served as National Treasurer of the National Political Congress of Black Women for eight years and the Secretary of the Collective Banking Group Inc. of Prince George's County Maryland for ten years.

Reverend Dr. Miller Perrin served for four years as the Chief of Staff/Senior Assistant to the Senior Minister at the historic Metropolitan Baptist Church in Washington, DC for four years. In that position she had management and supervisory authority over the administrative, programmatic, and organizational life of the church. She was charged to ensure that every aspect of the church life was managed and maintained at the highest level of professional excellence.

Reverend Dr. Miller Perrin is currently serving as an Associate Pastor at the First Baptist Church of Glenarden, in Landover, Maryland, under the leadership of Pastor John K. Jenkins Sr. She received the Doctor of Ministry degree from Regent University in Virginia Beach, Virginia. She is a Certified Life Coach.

For Bookings & More Information Visit: leadersraisingthebar.com

Endnotes

1. 1 Tim 4:12 (NKJV)
2. Comprehensive Etymological Dictionary of the English Language, London, England Elsevier, 1967.
3. B. M. Bass, R. M. Stogdills, Handbook of Leadership: Theory, Research, & Management Applications, (New York: The Free Press 1990), 100.
4. Warren Bennis. On Being a Leader. Reading Mass: Addison Wesley, 1994.
5. P. G. Northhouse, Leadership Theory and Practice (2nd Ed.) Thousand Oaks, Sage Publication (2001)
6. Acts 20:2
7. Mark A. Billings: Napoleon A French Leader
8. M. Webber, The Theory of Social and Economic Organization. Trans. By A.M. Henderson and T. Parsons. (New York: FREE Press. 1947), 40.
9. B. M. Bass, *Leadership and Performance Beyond Expectations* (New York: Free Press 1985) , 121.
10. James Burns, *Leadership, Leadership* (New York: Harper & Row 1978) 45.
11. Ibid, 46.
12. Hans Finzel, *The Top Ten Mistakes Leaders Make*, (David C. Cook, Colorado, Spring, CO 2007) 33.
13. Aubrey Malphurs, *Being Leaders: The Nature of Authentic Christian Leadership*, (Baker Books, 2007) 31.
14. Frank Luthans and Bruce Avolio , *Authentic Leadership Development Positive Organization*: Scholarship Foundation of a New Discipline,(San Francisco, Calif. (Berrett -Koehler Published 2003)

15. Shamir, B.G. Eilam. "What's Your Story? A Life story approach to Authentic Leadership Development," *The Leadership Quarterly* (Winter 2005), 98.

16.www.psychologytoday.com/us/blog/cutting-edge-leadership/201003/do-men-and-women-lead-differently-whos-better

17. Ibid

18. 1 Cor. 14:34

19. Vashti McKenzie, *Not Without a Struggle: Leadership Development for African American In Ministry*. Cleveland, United Church Press 1996.

20. Dr. Estrelda Alexander and Amos Young, eds., *Phillip's Daughters Women in Pentecostal-Charismatic Leadership*. (Eugene, OR: Pickwick Publication 2009) 45.

21. https://wliut.com/women-in-leadership-davinci/

22. Bruce Avolio, "Unlocking the Mask: A Look at the process by which Authentic Leaders Impact Followers Attitudes and Behavior," Leadership Quarterly, 15 (6) (Summer 2004) 801-823.

23. Ibid

24. Ibid.

25. Michael Kernis, "A Multicomponent Conceptualization of Authenticity: Theory and Research" Advance in Experimental Psychology, 2006

26. Simon Sinek, SUCCESS Magazine, *We are Better Together*, Audio CD December 2016.

27. Brown, R, *The Gift of Imperfection: Let Go of Who You Think You're Supposed to be Embrace Who You Are.*

28. Howard Thurman; *The Inward Journey: Meditations on the Spiritual Quest.*

29. John 10:27 (NKJV)

30. Bob Rue, *Value-based Leadership – Determining Our Personal Values, Senior Behavioral Sciences for Hanscom Air Force Base*, Bedford Mass.

31. Jim Collins – *Good to Great: Why Some Companies Make the Leap and Others Don't.* (New York: Harper Business 2001).

32. https://www.inc.com/marissa-levin/reading-habits-of-the-most-successful-leaders-that.html
33. Genesis 2:18
34. Peter F. Drucker, *In Leader of the Future*, ed. Hesselbein et al., xii.
35. David Gergen, *Eyewitness to Power: The Essence of Leadership Nixon to Clinton*, New York: Simon & Schuster 2000.
36. Acts 2:42 NKJV
37. John Maxwell, Developing the Leaders Around you: How to help Others Reach their Full Potential, Nashville, Tenn. 1995.
38. Dr. Joseph Umidi, Transformational Coaching, Virginia Beach, Wulon Press, 2004.
39. George William, Authentic Leadership: Recovering the Secrets to Creating Lasting Value (San Francisco, Jossey-Bass 2003), 23.
40. Patrick Lencioni, *Getting Naked: A Business Fable About Shedding the Three Fears That Sabotage Client Loyalty*, San Francisco, California, Published Jossey-Bass, 2010) vii
41. Brene' Brown, *Daring Greatly; How the Courage to Be Vulnerable Transforms the Way We Live, Love, Parent and Lead.* New York, New York Penguin Random House, 2012, 34
42. Bill George, *True North; Discover Your Authentic Leadership*, San Francisco, CA: Published by Jossey-Bass, 2007, 81.
43. Peter Scazzero, *The Emotionally Healthy Church; A Strategy for Discipleship that Actually Changes Lives.* Zondervan, Grand Rapids, Michigan, 2010, 127
44. M. Scott Boren, *The Relational Way; From Small Group Structures and Holistic Life*
45. Galatians 6:1 NCV
46. Thomas Lickona introduced us to this anonymous verse in a lecture he delivered at Santa Clara University's Markkula Center for Applied Ethics, 2/22/2001.

47. Norman Schwarzkopf, United States Army General, 25 Quotes, www.azquotes.com

48. Character; www. Reference.com

49. Williams George, *Find your Voice. (*Harvard Business Review, 2004.)

50. S. Michie and J. Gooty, *Values, Emotions, and Authenticity: Will the Real Leaders Please Stand up?* (The Leadership Quarterly 2005.)

51. Stephen M.R. Covey, The Speed of Trust (New York, FREE PRESS), 2006, 2018.

52. Colin Powell, *It worked For Me: In life and Leadership*, (HarperCollins, 2012).

53. R.C. Mayer. Trust in management and performance: Who minds the shop while the employees watch the boss? Academy of Management Journal 2005.

54. Patrick Lencioni, *The Advantage: Why Organizational Health Trumps Everything Else in Business, (Jossey-Bass 2012)*

55. James M. Kouzes and Barry Z. Posner, *Credibility, How Leaders Gain and Lose it, Why People Demand it?* (Jossey-Bass, Sans Francisco, California. 2011)

56. M.R. Covey, *The Speed of Trust* (New York Free Press 2006).

57. Stephen R. Covey, *Principle-Centered Leadership* (New York: Simon & Schuster 1991).

58. George Barna, *Leaders on Leadership* (California: Baker Publishing 1998).

59. James M. Kouzes and Barry Z. Posner, *Credibility; How Leaders Gain and Lose it, Why People Demand it?* (Jossey-Bass, Sans Francisco, California. 2011, page 5.

60. Stephen L. Carter, *Integrity* (New York: Harper Collins 1996).

61. Integrity (2008) Encarata http://encarta.msn.com/encnet/features/dictionary/dictioaryhome. Aspax. Accessed.

62. Stephen Carter, *Integrity* (New York: Harper Collins 1996).

63. John Maxwell, *Developing the Leaders Around you: How to help others Reach Their Full Potential* (Nashville, 1995.)

64. The Clear Word Bible; 2 Corinthians 8:21.

65. Stephen R. Covey, *Principles -Centered Leadership*, "Give a man a fish and you feed him for a day; teach him how to fish and you feed him for a Lifetime." (Simon & Schuster, 1990).

66. So-Young Kang, *The True Meaning of Integrity*, CEO@Gnowbe, Catalyst@ Awaken Group, updated December 2017.

67. P. Palmer, *Leading from Within*, L.C. Spears (Ed.) Insights on Leadership: Service, Spirit and Servant Leadership (New York: John Wiley) 1988, 197.

68. Ethics & Integrity in Business, University of Notre Dame, Mendoza College of Business 2011.

69. T. Cunningham, Leadership 101, Integrity. Retrieved March 2019 from http://withthecomman.com

70. Cheating in College, Karen Farkas, https://articles.ceveland.com/metro/index.ssf2017/cheating _in_college. Retrieve March 2019.

71. Emery P. Dalesio, Duke University pays $112 M to settle faked-research lawsuit, www.apnews.com retrieved March 25, 2019..

72. https://ethicalleadership.nd.edu/news/go-ahead-get-angry-about-unethical-behavior. Retrieved March 2019.

73. Loyalty Encarta http://Encarta. Sn.com/encnet/features/dictionary /dictionaryhome.aspx (accessed September 15, 2019).

74. Mary Miller, *Transformational Leadership and Mutuality*, Transformation View (2007) page 3-4.

75. Ted W. Engstrom, *The Making of a Christian Leader: How to Develop Management and Human Relationships Skills*, (Grand Rapids, Zondervan Publisher 1976), 86.

76. Mentalfloss.com, New Guideline Redefines Birth Years for Millennials, Gen-X and Post Millennials, 2018.

77. Bruce Winston: *Be A Leader for God's Sake* (Virginia Beach, Va. Regent University; School of Leadership Studies 2002).

78. www. Fortune.com/2015 Know your Millennial Co Workers.

79. J. Kouzes and B. Posner, *Credibility: How Leaders Gain and Lose It; Why People Demand* It (Jossey-Bass, San Francisco, Ca. 2011) 9.

80. NIV New Leadership Bible, Romans 12:2.

81. Peter Scazzero, *The Emotionally Healthy Church: A Strategy for Discipleship that Actually Changes Lives* (Grand Rapids, Zondervan, 2010).

82. Peter Scazzero, *The Emotionally Healthy Church: A Strategy for Disciples that Actually Changes Lives* (Grand Rapids: Zondervan, 2010).

83. Travis Bradberry & Jean Greaves, *Emotional Intelligence* 2.0 (San Diego, TalentSmart) 2009).

84. Daniel Goleman, Richard Boyatzis, and Annie McKee, *Primal leadership; Learning to Lead with Emotional Intelligence,* (Boston, Harvard Business School Press 2004).

85. S. Michie and J. Gooty *Values, Emotion and Authenticity: Will the Real Leader Please Stand Up?* The Leadership Quarterly, 16, 2005).

86. John 10:10

87. Romans 3:10

88. Jeremiah 17:9

Made in the
USA
Columbia, SC